YOUR
EXTRAORDINARY WHY

Endorsements

"In *Your Extraordinary Why*, and in his inspiring TEDx Talk, Brett Pyle captures the essence of Viktor Frankl's ideas about the human capacity of finding *meaning* and *significance* in life and conveys them most accurately – and lively."

Prof. Dr. Franz J. Vesely
University of Vienna &
The Viktor Frankl Institute

"Brett Pyle is one of the most sought-after speakers in the Vistage community. Every year he speaks to thousands of our CEO and business owner members, helping them find meaningful purpose in their lives. In *Your Extraordinary Why*, Brett brings to life some of his most valuable concepts as he challenges us all to live a legendary life. For anyone who is blessed with the opportunity to lead, Brett's book will be a key ingredient to becoming more effective while learning to enjoy the journey along the way. Powerful lessons, crisp insights, and opportunities for positive reflection make this an inspiring read. Read this book, move powerfully forward in life and business, and create your own exciting legacy!"

Sam Reese
CEO – Vistage Worldwide
The world's largest CEO development organization

"This book is the blueprint you've been looking for if you've ever pondered life's bigger questions: *Why do I do what I do? How can I make a difference? What's my purpose?* The book is even more important if you've *never* asked those questions. Brett shows you the way, right from the compelling opening story. Read and you'll learn all about "the *whys* behind your *whats*" to discover your own *Extraordinary Why*. I had the profound experience of hearing Brett deliver the "live" version of this book – it was transformational. I'm impressed at how well he now conveys his powerful performance into a book that packs the same punch. Accept Brett's *"Invitation to Make Your Life Extraordinary!"* You'll be glad you did!"

Maura Nevel Thomas
Inc "Top Leadership" Speaker, Author of 3 Books
Contributor to *HBR*, *Entrepreneur* & *Huffington Post*

Endorsements

"Brett Pyle's *Your Extraordinary Why* workshop is a remarkable blend of soulful reflection and performance art. In this book, the playwright and performer shares his 'script' and motivation to the reader's profound benefit. Each of us inherently enters the world with a purpose and a promise yearning for ever-fuller expression called significance. If you don't think your life matters and makes a difference, think again by reading Brett's book. You'll be uplifted and challenged to be more authentically who you really are."

Kevin W. McCarthy
Author, *The On-Purpose Person, Making Your Life Make Sense*
Chief Leadership Officer, On-Purpose Partner

"With a masterful eye, keenly focused on what matters, Brett takes us into the very depth of our purpose for being on the planet. Be prepared to be distracted from your daily routine and find yourself ruminating on questions that, today more than ever, the world needs us to answer for ourselves. Captivating storytelling makes the content accessible and this book hard to put down!"

I. Barry Goldberg
Executive Coach, Professional Speaker
Leadership Development Specialist

"In *Your Extraordinary Why* we now have a book that, like Brett's workshop, is not just a little life changing, it's transformational! The moment you start reading you'll want to live a life of significance by discovering and expressing your *extraordinary why*. Read to the very end, and you'll discover how!"

Patty Vogan Geyer
Spiritual Leadership Coach
Author, Professional Speaker

"This book will entertain, inspire, confront, and challenge you. But most importantly, it will empower you to contribute your unique verse to life's powerful play."

Don Oglesby
President/CEO – Homes of Hope

Endorsements

"Not many inspire an understanding of the significance of a life of purpose better than Brett Pyle – through his inspirational programs, and now in his wonderful book. Here, he offers us a way of seeing life as a journey made divine by the value, service, and purpose we invest in it. Read *Your Extraordinary Why* and you'll discover how extraordinary you are – particularly when you infuse your existence with purpose and the desire to give meaning to your legacy."

Ben Dominitz
Vistage Chair, Strategic Advisor, Servant Leader

"In his new book, *Your Extraordinary Why*, Brett Pyle challenges us to stop thinking about short-term goals and instead focus on the long-term goals that will generate lasting significance. A must-read for anyone feeling overworked, overwhelmed, and longing for a more fulfilling way to live and work. Perfect for individual exploration and ideally suited for CEOs and leaders who want to harness the power of WHY in their organization."

Cathy Fyock, CSP, SPHR, SHRM-SCP
Bestselling Author – *The Speaker Author*

"Brett Pyle has done the research, walked with extraordinary people, and is willing to openly show you the reality of what it takes to be extraordinary based on his own journey. This book will help you develop a natural, manageable, intensive relationship with *the force* that will create in you the extraordinary person you are meant to be. Prepare to be extraordinarily real."

Chuck Reeves, CSP, CPAE
Author, Speaker, Sales Developer

"In *Your Extraordinary Why*, Brett Pyle transcribes his vast expertise connecting people to their purpose to the written page. If finding meaning and creating a legacy of significance within your success is important to you, this book should take a top spot on your 'must read' list."

Steve Lorch
Author, Entrepreneur
Founder, Table Rock Tea Company

Endorsements

"*Your Extraordinary Why* oozes with Brett's unique style and charm and captures the magic of his message. Whether you're lucky enough to have experienced one of Brett's programs or are just stumbling upon his work for the first time, you're sure to find this book to be a resource you'll return to time and again. Packed with paradigm-shifting perspectives, and life-changing insights, *Your Extraordinary Why* should be a staple for every leader's bookshelf."

Rebecca Heiss, PhD
Professional Speaker & Self-Awareness Expert
Author, *Instinct*

"*Your Extraordinary Why* is a compelling *must read* for everyone who wants their life to matter. Brett delivered his signature workshop, upon which this book is based, at my annual Leadership Evolution Conference. Rare is the individual that can captivate a large audience for a full 6 hours. Brett did and received rave reviews! A master storyteller and thinker, Brett helped me, and my audience, connect directly with 'True North' on our compasses – through this book, he can help you find yours!"

John Dame
Leadership Coach, Author
Business Strategist

"*Your Extraordinary Why* is an invaluable resource for anyone who wants to live a meaningful, significant, extraordinary life!"

H. Skip Weitzen
Author, *Hypergrowth* & *Infopreneurs*

"Get ready to go on a journey. *Your Extraordinary Why* will challenge your thinking, stretch your soul, and warm your heart. Brett Pyle is a gifted messenger, doing the important work of waking us all up. *Your Extraordinary Why* is a roadmap to our highest calling, our deepest values, our strongest love. Read this at your own risk – you will never be the same."

Irina Baranov, CPCC
Vistage Master Chair,
Executive Coach, Speaker/Facilitator

Endorsements

"Brett Pyle is a wonderful leader and world class teacher. In *Your Extraordinary Why*, he proves himself a masterful author, as well. His engaging storytelling, thoughtful examples, and conversational style will have you fully engrossed while flipping pages and will inspire you to embrace the limitless possibility that remains alive and well within your story. Seize the opportunity to elevate your life by reading this book. Not only will you be better for it, so will those you profoundly impact as a result of it."

John O'Leary
#1 National Bestselling Author of *On Fire,* and *IN AWE*
Host of the *Live Inspired* Podcast

"Today's world is in desperate need of moral leadership – competent, virtuous, trusted leaders of deep character and clarity of purpose. To become such an extraordinary leader who transforms the world, you must first experience profound transformation for yourself. If you're already on the journey, Brett's book will help you progress. If you've been waiting to get started – *carpe diem!* You only get one chance to leave the legacy you were born to deliver to the world. Read *Your Extraordinary Why* and seize the day!"

Richard S. Lytle, Ph.D.
President & CEO, The CEO Forum, Inc.

"I have seen God use Brett Pyle to help people experience major breakthroughs in their thinking, problem solving, and spiritual insight. Whenever I know Brett is coaching someone or speaking at an event, I am confident that the people will be deeply impacted as a result. That is why I am so excited about his book, *Your Extraordinary Why*. It encapsulates his popular teaching and makes it readily accessible to anyone who wants to live a more focused, purposeful, and rewarding life."

Richard Blackaby, PhD
President Blackaby Ministries International
Co-Author, *Experiencing God, Spiritual Leadership Coaching*

YOUR EXTRAORDINARY WHY

LIVING A SUCCESSFUL LIFE OF SIGNIFICANCE

Brett Pyle

Your Extraordinary Why – Living a Life of Successful Significance
Copyright © 2020 by Brett Pyle.

ISBN – 978-1-7340715-0-4 (Paperback)

Cover designed by Kenneth Overman

Printed in the United States of America

First Printing: February 2020

Published by Brett Pyle

www.brettpyle.com

This publication is designed to provide accurate and authoritative information in regard to the subject matter covered. It is sold with the understanding that neither the author nor the publisher is engaged in rendering legal, accounting, securities trading, psychological, or other such professional services. If legal advice or other expert assistance is required, the services of a competent professional person should be sought.

— Adapted from a Declaration of Principles
Jointly Adopted by Committees of
Publishers, Authors, Associations,
& The American Bar Association

Contents

Acknowledgments

There's an old African Proverb: *"If you want to go fast, go alone. If you want to go far, go together."* It's of uncertain origin and has probably been quoted to the point of cliché, but it certainly holds true in the creation of this book that's been five years in the making. I would, therefore, be remiss if I didn't take time to acknowledge and thank the many contributors to this effort. Hopefully, this book's impact will *'go far'* because of our collaboration.

First, I owe many thanks to the members of the three Vistage Boards I chaired and coached for the past decade. You were the first ones to encourage me to share this message more broadly with the world. It was the day John O'Leary spoke to our Boards that I first committed, out loud, to speak professionally. So, thank you, John, for demonstrating the power of the spoken word to compel a leader into purpose-driven action.

Dr. Richard Blackaby – You personify obedience to a 'call,' and a life well, and faithfully, lived. Thank you for believing in me when I doubted God's presence and inspiring me to speak and write about my experiences. I'm often humbled when I reflect on all that God has done through the *Spiritual Leadership Coaching* practice He placed on your heart all those years ago. Thanks for inviting me to join you, and our magnificent Creator, on that experience!

Rachel Hamilton Huffman, my Chief Editor & Encourager – We started this journey together five years ago. I'm grateful for your much-needed grammar skills, your editorial and self-publishing wisdom, and your patience with me throughout the many arduous parts of the authoring process.

Kaitlyn Pyle – Thank you for the countless hours you invested bringing my visions to life. Your delightful black & white illustrations add much color to my stories and give soul to this book. Your gifts are bountiful – thank you for sharing a few of them with my readers.

Acknowledgments

My good friend, Steve Lorch – you've gone *'All-In'* more times than anyone I know. I've been the beneficiary of your sage wisdom and guidance on occasions too numerous to count. You're the Spock to my Kirk, the friend that sticks closer than any brother. Words are insufficient.

Thanks to my sister, the brilliant Pamela Viktoria Pyle, for your editorial review and honest feedback. You're the bravest person I know – Mom & Dad would be very proud of you!

My gratitude goes out to Prof. Franz J. Vesely, Ph.D for your editorial reviews of my descriptions of Viktor's Frankl's life and work. I'm honored you took the time to view my TEDx Talk. Thank you for encouraging me to continue speaking and to complete this book. The work that you, and all those affiliated with *The Viktor Frankl Institute* in Vienna, Austria (www.viktorfrankl.org), do to teach the world about Logotherapy is deeply important, today more than ever.

Thank you, Alex Vesely, for compellingly telling Viktor's story in your artfully produced movie *Viktor & I*. I'm incredibly grateful you took my phone call and were supportive of my portrayal of the significance of your grandfather's work and meaning to the world. He was a great man who clearly found and lived from his *Extraordinary Why!*

Thanks to the dedicated staff and curators at the Nobel Museum in Stockholm, Sweden and the Nobel Peace Center in Oslo, Norway. I appreciate the time you invested answering all my questions and helping me understand the life and motivations of Alfred Nobel.

Thanks to student leaders at Grand Canyon University who ran the *Magnus Opus* TEDx event in 2018. You sought me out to participate at a time when others were rejecting my message. Our faith stories intersected that day. We all learned a great deal about connecting to, and leading from, a purpose larger than ourselves in the process.

Acknowledgments

Thanks to my inspirational colleagues at the National Speakers Association. Our close association has been instrumental in bringing this work to fruition and has helped me join the ranks of becoming a Speaker Author.

David Setzer – We've learned so much together over the years. When are we going to write our book and tell our story? Thanks for 'doing life' with me.

My deepest gratitude to hundreds of Vistage Chairs and thousands of Vistage Members around the world who've given me the opportunity to develop this message by speaking it to you in my workshops. You've helped me find *my voice* and have given me a platform from which to express it. Thank you. Together, we are making a significant difference in the world!

Finally, I must thank those influential family members in my lineage who constitute my *spiritual heritage*. My mom, Victoria K. Pyle and my dad, Thomas A. Pyle – I know you would be very proud to see this work in print. Thanks also to my grandfather and grandmother Thomas Virgil & Evelyn B. Pyle; my great uncle Gov. Howard Pyle, and my great-grandfather, Rev. Thomas Miller Pyle. Collectively, you formed the crucible in which I was forged. This story was birthed in you generations ago. I hope I'm found to have stewarded it faithfully when I eventually join you all in eternity – hopefully not too soon!

Dedication

To Jeanne, my wife, the love of my life – you are the manifestation of God's inexplicable, unconditional, love for me! You are not my *Extraordinary Why*, but *He* most assuredly gave you to me as His perfect gift of love and grace. Where would I be without you?

To my children: Lauren, who made and taught me to be a father, and still calls me 'Daddy;' Kaitlyn, who makes me laugh and keeps me endlessly entertained; and Jonathan, who continues to teach me what it means to have, and love, a wonderful Son – not just be saved by one. Thank you all for filling my life with wonder, joy, and amazement!

Do not grow weary in doing good, my dear ones. Keep on living and leading from your *Extraordinary Whys* – share *your voices* with a world in desperate need of them.

Introduction

Your Life and Legacy

"It is all a journey.
We are all on a journey filled with gifts."
— Kevin Hall, Aspire

The journey of *your* lifetime!

Come with me on a journey. The journey of *your* lifetime!

It's an epic journey! So, let's make sure we get started in the right direction. On the count of three, from wherever you are right now, point in the direction of Paris, France.

Ready? One ... two ... three ... point.

Are you right? Who knows? It doesn't really matter. This is a journey of imagination.

Now, look up above your pointed finger.

Set your gaze on the horizon and picture Paris, France in your mind.

Are you there? *Visualize* Paris in your mind's eye as we go back in time:

Paris, France. April 1888.

Early morning dew glistens on the exposed skin of your arm. Men and women like you are just rising. They're heading off to work, school, and various other endeavors of a sure-to-be-full day ahead. In the street below, you hear the sound of horse-drawn carriages. One is stuck in the rain-soaked mud – April in Paris is very wet.

Can you picture it? Can you hear it?

Ahh … Paris in the springtime!

Now, take a deep breath.

Fill your lungs completely. Breathe in this moist, early morning air. Immediately, you detect a distinct aroma: fresh-baked bread rising from the boulangerie, the bakery, below. They're baking croissants and baguettes that Parisians will gobble up for breakfast, lunch, and dinner. This city loves her bread!

Now, keeping your eyes out in the distance, rotate your head 45 degrees clockwise to the right. There on the horizon are the diagonally crisscrossed steel girders of a half-constructed Eiffel Tower emerging from the ground.

Construction began a year ago. It'll be another year before its completion for the opening of the Grand Exposition in 1889.

Are you there? Can you visualize it? Feel, hear, smell, and taste it? Is it *palpable*? I hope so. The more of yourself you bring to this journey, the greater impact it will have on you.

Here you are in Paris, France, April 1888.

This was the setting that greeted a 55-year-old Alfred Nobel. He sat at his rooftop café that morning, drinking his steaming hot espresso, eating his buttery croissant, reading his morning newspaper.

A headline caught his eye.

For you French speakers, the headline read:

"Le Marchand de la Mort est Mort!"

For the rest of us:

"The Merchant of Death is Dead!"

Provocative. He decides to read on and quickly discovers it's no ordinary headline. It's an obituary. Turns out, it wasn't any 'run-of-the-mill' obituary either.

It was *HIS* obituary!

Alfred was in town this particular day because, the week before, his older brother Ludwig had passed away. Alfred came to attend the funeral. It wasn't unusual that the French newspaper had both men's obituaries prepared and ready to print. They were two of the world's five wealthiest men, and they were getting on in years. So, the papers were ready.

Sadly, mistakenly, the French newspaper selected the wrong man's pre-prepared obituary, printing Alfred's instead of Ludwig's.

Now, with great interest, Alfred reads:

Le Marchand de la Mort est Mort!

Alfred Nobel made his fortune by inventing faster and more efficient means of killing men than ever before. Through his invention of Dynamite, he literally created modern warfare.

Finally, at last, the Merchant of Death is dead!

Alfred got a glimpse of the *legacy* he would one day leave to the world. The poor man was, literally, mortified.

It was kind of a raw deal too. The invention of dynamite was the achievement of a goal, the culmination of immense work and effort.

It was a significant goal – one Nobel intentionally set out to achieve. He was proud of his accomplishment. More than that, the reason driving him to accomplish this goal was deeply meaningful. It was personal. In fact, Alfred's motivation, the *why behind his what*, was even bigger than the goal itself.

When Alfred was a younger man, his younger brother, Emil, was killed in the family business. Alfred's father, an inventor, started a business manufacturing a compound called nitroglycerine.

Many believe nitroglycerine was used in warfare. But, was it?

No. Actually, it's not very useful in battle because it's too unstable. Shake it. Apply too much pressure or allow the temperature to vary too much and it will explode. You yourself get killed on the way to the battlefield – not a very wise strategy or useful weapon. You'd prefer that your enemies attempt to use it!

This was exactly what happened on September 3rd, 1864 at the Heleneborg Estate, just outside of Stockholm, Sweden. On that day, 21-year old Emil Nobel, two other employees, and two passersby were all killed. A company laboratory in which nitroglycerine was being manufactured exploded.

On that date in Alfred's young life, he declared to himself: 'NO!'

"No. There has to be a safer, more stable compound than nitroglycerine so that people like my brother don't needlessly perish."

Construction, Civil Engineering, Mining – these were the primary industries their company served. Building up the infrastructure for burgeoning 19th Century Europe. Not primarily warfare.

Three years later, in 1867, Noble received U.S. patent number 78,317 for a new invention. In total, Nobel would ultimately earn 355 patents attributed to his name. One man. 355 patents. Wow! That's quite an accomplishment in a single life. This one, #78317, was for a stabilized nitroglycerine compound he called *Dynamite* – safe, light, easily transportable. So stable it won't blow up unless a blasting cap, another Nobel patent, is inserted into it.

Dynamite: the ultimate embodiment of a goal he set out to achieve!

Nobel also made value-based decisions of integrity along his corporate journey. Another of those 355 patents was for a compound called Gelignite. Ever hear of it? Probably not … for good reason.

Gelignite was definitely an improvement on Dynamite – it was 10x more powerful. Yet, Nobel considered the need in the industries he served and concluded that dynamite was getting the job done. It was strong enough. The world didn't need Gelignite.

So, he took this new invention, as innovative and powerful as it was, and put it on the shelf. He never monetized this one. He could have sold it to the military along with dynamite. Foreign militaries clamored for the formula. Instead, he intentionally chose *not* to release it.

So, on that early Parisian morning in April 1888, Alfred Nobel thought to himself:

Let's get this straight: I set a big, worthy goal. I executed it expertly. I made value-based, intentional decisions of integrity along life's journey. Now here, at age 55, I'm being eulogized as 'the Merchant of Death who created faster and more efficient ways of killing men than ever before!'

Argh! The very thought ticked him off!

That's NOT who I am. This is most certainly NOT the way I want to be remembered.

After some deep reflection that April morning, Nobel resolved to change this aspect of his legacy. He intentionally set out to do so.

He became an outspoken advocate for Peace. In 1891, he said to a dear friend, Austrian peace activist, Countess Bertha von Suttern:

"My dynamite will sooner lead to peace than a thousand world conventions. As soon as men will find that in one instant, whole armies can be utterly destroyed, they surely will abide by golden peace."

In the end, it's true that Nobel's explosives were used for destructive purposes in warfare. But, much more frequently, they were used for constructive, peaceful purposes. Nobel's inventions were used to create railways and roadways, buildings and bridges, hydroelectric dams and power stations. The man was quite the paradox, really. An explosives manufacturer – staunchly committed to peace!

Nobel eventually passes away of a stroke on December 10[ii], 1896. When his will[ii] is opened, the world is surprised to discover he's chosen to leave 97% of his fortune, 31 million Swedish Kroner (about half a billion US$, today) to establish and fund The Nobel Prizes.

Nobel instituted five specific prizes: Peace, Physics, Chemistry, Medicine, and Literature (Economics would be added later) to recognize and honor **"those who, during the preceding year, shall have conferred the greatest benefit to mankind."**

Today, when most think of the Nobel name, they think more about the prizes in general. For most of us, it's the Nobel *Peace* Prize that specifically comes to mind. This one Nobel established to honor *"the person who shall have done the most or the best work for fraternity between nations, for the abolition or reduction of standing armies and for the holding and promotion of peace congresses."*

This seems to be true, even if we have heard some version of this complex man's paradoxical story.

Nobel's story makes it clear:

> *You CAN be intentional and take charge of your Legacy!*
> IF you want to – AND, IF you just happen to have half a billion $US at your disposal!

As we consider Nobel's legacy shift, questions remain: *Why* would *you* want to change *your* legacy? *Why* should you care about what people think or say about you after your passing? After all, you're going to be gone anyway! Isn't this all a bit self-indulgent?

How you'll be remembered and why it matters

Eulogy. Legacy.

Nobel's story touched on both concepts. Take a moment to think about those words. What do they mean? Are these the same thing or are they different?

If you said, 'the same,' you're partially right. Both describe a person's life after they're gone. So, in that regard, there are certainly elements of similarity that link these words.

But if you said, 'they're different,' you're also right!

When and where will your eulogy exist? At *a moment in time* – your funeral. When and where will your legacy live? Also in the future – but not just at the funeral. Your legacy will live in the hearts and minds of *other* people, *continuously*, whenever you come to their minds.

That's fascinating isn't it? Your *Legacy*, the single most personal thing you're creating while you're here on Earth, isn't yours at all – it belongs to other people!

Eulogy. Any idea where that word comes from?

eulogy
[**yoo**-l*uh*-jee]

Eulogy comes from two Greek root words: Eu – the same root word in the word *euphoria*, the 'good feelings' we get from time to time. So, Eu means 'good.' Then we have -logy, logia, or logos, meaning 'the study of,' 'speech,' or, more simply, 'words.'

Put these together: Eu-logy: "The Good Words." The name for the speech delivered at a funeral.

Of course, that's consistent with a phrase we've known all our lives:

'It's not kind to speak ill of the dead.'

Is it? Of course not! So, we don't. At least, not initially. We give it some time; then, we tell the world what we *really* thought of the individual. That's when our *legacy* truly starts to emerge.

legacy
[**leg**-*uh*-see]

Our *Legacy* is what we will leave to future generations. It isn't *just* the good words. It's the good, the bad, and the ugly.

Our *Legacy* is the totality of the impact we had on the world while we were in it. Especially, the impact we had on those who knew us most closely – those most likely to remember us at all.

Pause to think about this for just a moment:

> *Your legacy is the sum total of the blessings, and curses, you'll leave behind for future generations.*

Your legacy is not just the impact you'll have on the next generation, but on many generations to come. The choices you made yesterday; the ones you'll make today and tomorrow, can, and will, impact future generations – for better (blessings) or for worse (curses). That's deep stuff to ponder!

Clearly, Alfred Nobel left both blessings and curses to the world that survived him. In April 1888, eight years before he would die, he received the gift of getting a glimpse of his *legacy* in advance.

Not surprisingly, his legacy was taking shape around one of the significant goals he set and accomplished. Specifically, it was the invention of dynamite that was about to define his legacy.

Then, Nobel actively worked to shift his legacy to center on another one of his goals: The Peace Prize.

So too, in no small part, *your legacy* will be defined by the goals you set and achieve while you're here on earth. The 'stuff you do' while you're here on earth.

Goals – What we achieve shapes our legacy

I know this sounds like a basic question, but have you ever set out to accomplish something? Anything?

If so, then you're a goal setter.

You might not write down specific goals. You might not intentionally plan and drive toward the achievement of clearly articulated goals. Nevertheless, you are probably a goal setter to some degree or another.

That's why you picked up this book, for example. Perhaps the title caught your eye. The material seemed related to some thoughts you've been having, and you decided: "I'm going to read this."

Even a decision as small as that is a goal. We set goals all the time. Why?

Firstly, it feels good to set and achieve a goal, doesn't it? Something seems meaningful to you; you decide you're going to pursue it; you work really hard; you achieve the goal; and it *feels* good! We tend to get *euphoric* feelings when we set and achieve goals. It's satisfying!

Goal setting is also powerful. It's an act of faith. When we set goals, we set into motion a *spiritual* dynamic. *What* we set out to achieve isn't a physical reality at the time we set the goal. It comes to exist first in our minds. Then we speak it aloud, and *then* it comes into physical reality.

That's the creative process. It's part of our powerful human nature. When we act in accord with our creative nature and achieve something, it *feels* good. Creation is tied into the core of *who* we are as human beings. That's why goal setting, and achievement, is *usually* satisfying!

On the other hand, have you ever set a goal that seemed meaningful to you at the time you set it? You work really hard. You achieve it! But when you do, the sensation is more like: *"Huh! Is that all there is?"*

Somehow or another, the achievement of the goal went unnoticed. Unappreciated. Perhaps it left you wanting or unsatisfied?

'Why did I do that? That wasn't all I was hoping it would be.'

Financial goals often fall into this category. There is an urban myth that when John D. Rockefeller was the wealthiest man in the world, he was interviewed:

'Mr. Rockefeller. You've amassed more wealth than anyone currently living. Surely, you're qualified to answer this question: Just exactly how much money does it take to satisfy a person?'

His answer? *'Just a little bit more than he has, son. Just a dollar more!'*

The story is unverified but the message rings true. Just exactly *how much more* money is necessary to satisfy a person, is open to debate,[iii] but the average answer seems to hover around 20% more than one currently has.

Test this figure for yourself. Pick the financial measure that means the most to you: Your annual salary? Your net worth? Your last bonus perhaps? Now, add ~20% to it and assume it's yours!

Pretty nice, huh? Satisfying?

Yes! I like that! Feels good!

Goals may, or may not, satisfy

The problem with that is, you may get 20% more. Then, let just a little time go by. Soon, you're going to want another 20%; then another; and so on. It becomes addictive, ultimately leaving you unsatisfied because it's always just out of grasp – a chasing after the wind.

So, is setting and pursuing financial goals a waste of time because they will *never* prove satisfying or fulfilling? No. Not not at all. That's not my point. Here's the lesson:

Work for money as your ultimate goal and you'll always be disappointed. Money is a wonderful servant, but a cruel master. *Master money or money will most assuredly master you.*

Please don't misunderstand: money, itself, even the pursuit of a financial goal, is not necessarily 'bad' or inappropriate. It's usually neutral. The goals we set in life, financial or otherwise, are *all* 'neutral.' Their achievement may, or may not, satisfy us personally.

It's really not the goals we pursue that ultimately matter to us. They're just the *whats* we go after.

> *It's the __why__ behind the __what__ that will dictate whether or not the achievement of your goals will ultimately fulfill you.*

If your *why* isn't big enough, if it isn't deep enough, if it isn't sufficiently connected to *who you are at your core*, to your *identity*, then when you achieve your goals, your *whats*, God help you!

Picture this: You're Alfred Nobel. It's December 1896 – you're lying on your deathbed. In that moment, you reflect on your life:

'So glad I invented faster and more efficient ways of killing people than ever before. I really nailed it there, didn't I?'

Ouch. Regret and remorse overwhelm you!

'What have I done?'

Now, go back to that same moment and reflect on your life like this:

'So glad I created a mechanism that led to the salvation of thousands of lives in the construction, civil engineering, and mining industries. The world is better because I was in it. I made a difference. I can go in peace.'

Same person, same moment, reflecting on exactly the same *what* – two distinctly different *whys*. One proves deeply fulfilling. Satisfying! The other – empty, wanting, regretful.

My first assertion of this book:

It's not the <u>whats</u> we set out to achieve that truly matter and lead to personal fulfillment.
Significance lies in the <u>whys</u> behind our whats.

What this book is all about

Think of your time in this book as a break from life, business, and your day-to-day existence. Time *to reflect on* your life, business, and your day-to-day existence.

Time to clarify the *big whys* in your life:

- Why am I doing any of the things I do in life? *Why?*

- What's really driving me on a day-to-day basis?

- Where do those big *whys* in my life come from?

- Do I need to reset my relationship with any of my driving *whys?*

Think of this book as:

> *Time away from your life,*
> *to reflect on your life,*
> *to make the most of your life.*

My second assertion at the outset of our journey:

> *You'll never fully grasp your biggest, deepest, most*
> *compelling whys —*
> *let alone your Extraordinary Why, your Purpose —*
> *until you come to grips with your one and only*
> *limited resource.*

What is that resource?

Time, of course. 60 seconds x 60 minutes x 24 hours x 365 days x however many years you may receive. That's it.

They're not adding any more grains of sand to that proverbial hourglass. The hands of your own personal Grandfather clock have been set. It's been fully wound, and it's winding down.

We don't get any more time.

Except, of course, every fourth year we get an extra day in February (LOVE the Leap Year) – very kind of the timekeepers!

AND every couple of years they add another second to the Astronomical clock, giving us Coordinated Universal Time (UTC). It's called a Leap Second. It makes some astrophysicist in Greenwich, England really happy (though it upsets every software developer). It accounts for the 23.5° tilt in our planet and the unpredictable slowing of earth's rotation.

Did you enjoy the last one? I got so much done – an extra sip of champagne on New Years' Eve 2016. Fantastic!

A few February 29[th]s – some occasional Leap Seconds.

But no. They're not making ... any ... more ... time.

Tick-Tock. Tick-Tock. Tick-Tock.

"Time takes it all, whether you want it to or not."
— The Green Mile[iv] *(The movie)*

NOTES

i. Kevin Hall. *Aspire: Discovering Your Purpose Through the Power of Words* (New York: HarperCollins Publishing, 2010).

ii. Levush, Ruth. "Alfred Nobel's Will: A Legal Document that Might Have Changed the World and a Man's Legacy." *Library of Congress.* Dec. 7, 2015. https://blogs.loc.gov/law/2015/12/alfred-nobels-will-a-legal-document-that-might-have-changed-the-world-and-a-mans-legacy/

iii. The Economics of Happiness Debate: Nobel prize-winning psychologist Daniel Kahneman, and economist Angus Deaton, concluded in a paper published by the Center for Health and Well-Being at Princeton University that in the United States, at least, happiness levels-off at incomes of around $75,000 a year. In other words, they suggest there's a wealth satiation point, or a threshold of wealth or income, that once reached, additional money won't necessarily increase happiness any further.

Counter to that point, however, in 2008, working for the National Bureau of Economic Research, Betsey Stevenson and Justin Wolfers, using a 2007 Gallup poll, found people with the highest incomes report the greatest degree of happiness and satisfaction with their lives. For instance, only 35% of people making less than $35,000 say they are "very happy," versus 100% of people making more than $500,000.

As Forbes Staff writer Susan Adams says in her May 10th, 2013 article *Money Does Buy Happiness, Says New Study*, "Using data on 155 countries from Gallup, the Pew Global Attitudes Survey, the World Bank and other sources, [Stevenson and Wolfers] found that as countries increase their GDP per capita, the more happiness levels rise. There is no point where that levels off. The richer people get, the more satisfied they are with their lives. "If there is a satiation point," they write, "we are yet to reach it."

This finding seems underscore Rockefeller's witty, and probably mythical, assertion with which we began.

Much more recently, Richard Easterlin asserted that "when asked how much more money they would need to be completely happy, people typically name a figure greater than their current income by about 20 percent."

A key concept in 'happiness economics' is called the Easterlin Paradox, named for USC economics professor Richard Easterlin who in 1974 theorized that within a country, richer people were usually happier than poorer people. The paradox being, however, he found no evidence to support that, on average at a national level, people in wealthier nations were any happier than people in poorer countries.

Easterlin, Richard A, "The Economics of Happiness." http://www-bcf-usc.edu/~easter/papers/Happiness/pdf; and *Does Economic Growth Improve the Human Lot? Some Empirical Evidence.* (New York: Academic Press, 1974), http://graphics8.nytimes.com/Images/2008/04/16/business/Easterlin1974.pdf

Betsey Stevenson, Justin Wolfers. "Economic Growth and Subjective Well-Being: Reassessing the Easterlin Paradox." The National Bureau of Economic Research. The Brookings Institution, 2008, http://www.nber.org/papers/w14 282.pdf

Susan Adams. "Money Does Buy Happiness, Says New Study." Forbes, 2008 https://www/forbes/com/sites/susanadams/2013/05/10/money-does-buy-happiness-says-new-study/#60dfa5ef615

Daniel Kahneman, Angus Deaton. "High income improves evaluation of life but not emotional well-being." *Proceedings of the National Academy of Sciences of the United States of America* 107, no. 38 (2010): https://www.pnas.org/content/pnas/107/38/16489.full.pdf

iv.   *The Green Mile,* directed by Frank Darabont (1999; Los Angeles, CA: Castle Rock Entertainment, Darkwoods Productions, Warner Bros. 2000), DVD.

Chapter 1

An Invitation to Make Your Life Extraordinary!

*"Time is what we want most,
but what we use worst."*
— *William Penn*

The Power of Drama

Three ... Two ... One ... Action!

I'm a movie fan. I was BORN a movie fan. I was born into a household with a Broadway actor and actress for parents. Mom and Dad actually met on stage in the 1956 Broadway musical *The Merry Widow*. Needless to say, there was quite a bit of 'drama' in my home! Even as a young kid, if I were given the choice between watching a sports game on TV or watching a movie, I *always* picked the movie. Didn't matter if Game 7 of the World Series, or even the Super Bowl, was playing – I'd always pick the film!

"Bond. James Bond." You could feel his icy stare!

"You call him 'Dr. Jones!'" Short Round admonished those who might presume to call his hero 'Indy!' Loved that little kid in the *'Temple of Doom'* prequel to *'Raiders of the Lost Ark!'*

"Hmmm. Strong The Force is with this one," mused our green guru Yoda. I literally *became* young Luke Skywalker and imagined that curious, wise mentor acknowledging my own strong, but undeveloped, gifts.

That's all it ever took, and I was hooked!

There's just something about an unfolding drama, an uncertain ending, that's spellbinding. It draws us in, keeps us guessing, fixed to the edge of our seats as we wonder how it's going to turn out. The suspense is captivating.

Yet, is the ultimate ending of such movies ever in doubt or does it just seem that way in the moment?

Somehow, because we know in our hearts that ultimately the hero saves the day and gets the girl (or boy), the tension becomes bearable no matter how dire the circumstances or intense the accompanying music.

There is still uncertainty, of course. That's drama! But behind it, there's hope, or faith, that all will be well in the end. So, as we watch these movies, the big questions in our minds evolve, enabling us to get through it all and actually enjoy the journey.

The question: "Will Bond defuse the bomb before it goes off or get blown to bits?"

Becomes: "HOW will Bond defuse the bomb?" Or, "How many seconds will be left on the timer *when* he does?"

Of course, we just *knew* the timer would read "007" when it stopped!

Yep. I'm definitely a movie fan. As such, I'm always watching films with an unusual degree of passionate curiosity. As a speaker, I'm always in search of film scenes that illustrate big life lessons in a powerful way – lessons that will *help connect people to their purpose* to become the very best leaders they were created to be.

Carpe diem!

Take, for example, the *life lesson* with which we ended the Introduction:

"TIME is our one and only limited resource."

Perhaps you've seen that moving, classic film, starring Robin Williams, *Dead Poet's Society.*[i] It's a coming-of-age film set in New England in the late 1950s.

Robin plays young Professor Keating, the newest English teacher at the Welton Academy for boys, a private, college-preparatory institution. Keating is no doubt a standout from his older, much more senior teaching peers. They are so very old, serious, strict, and boring! Keating is fun-loving, dynamic, and vibrant. Clearly, a role made for our beloved Robin Williams. Equally, Robin Williams, made the role.

In an early scene,[ii] on the first day of class, Professor Keating, whistling the 1812 Overture, marches all his boys out to the hallowed school foyer. There, he assigns a student the task of reading aloud the first stanza of a poem by 17th Century poet, Robert Herrick.

The young man obliges:

To the Virgins, to Make Much of Time

"Gather ye rosebuds while ye may,
Old Time is still a-flying;
And this same flower that smiles today
Tomorrow will be dying."

The student finishes and is thanked for his contribution. Keating repeats one of the lines from the poem and continues the lesson:

"'Gather ye rosebuds while ye may.' The Latin term for that sentiment is 'Carpe Diem.' Now who knows what that means?"

One bright student eagerly raises his hand and confidently answers: *"Carpe Diem. That's 'Seize the day!'"*

The boy smiles proudly as his teacher praises him for his response.

"Very good! Seize the day. 'Gather ye rose buds while ye may.' Why does the writer use these lines? Because we are food for worms, lads. Because, believe it or not ... each and every one of us in this room ... is one day, going to stop breathing. Turn cold. And die."

You can *feel* the tension in the air as the boys squirm uncomfortably. We, too, grow less comfortable as we contemplate our own mortality.

Professor Keating directs the boys' attention to a trophy case on the wall of the foyer. They stare into the case with its dark green velvet backdrop draped with victory ribbons; the weathered, leather pigskin footballs lining the case bottom; the old black-and-white photos of the school's sport heroes from a bygone age. Then, Keating invites the boys to lean in and listen to those faces whisper their legacy.

In unison, the boys physically lean in and angle their heads, ever so slightly, as if to give ear to the voices that perhaps they might hear.

After a long, dramatic pause, Keating eerily, and audibly, whispers:

"Carr – pe! Carpe Diem. Seize the day, lads!"

The camera zooms in and pans across the black and white faces of ghosts from the past. Keating concludes the scene with a final, commanding utterance:

*"**Make your lives extraordinary!**"*

Next, the camera cuts from the photos to the face of Professor Keating. Then, we focus on one of the students – a shy boy we'll soon come to know as young Mr. Anderson.

As the powerful scene fades to black, if we listen closely, we can hear a grandfather clock in the school foyer rhythmically ticking:

"Tick-tock. Tick-tock. Tick-tock."

You never actually *see* the clock; it's off-camera. Yet, it's there. Time is relentlessly marching on. The director reminds us of that fact, audibly, as we experience the scene, caught up in the moment along with the students.

That's drama!

Only Hollywood brings us such powerful scenes down to the smallest detail. In the film, the boys are hooked! So are we, thinking not so much about the boys' impending demise but our own. We are, indeed, 'food for worms,' are we not?

That hits close to home! It's personal. The most compelling sagas always are!

Personal – deeply personal.

So it will be on this journey. The journey of *your* lifetime as we travel together through this book.

You may wish to keep a journal in which you can write your thoughts as you read. Or, consider recording your reflections in the *Extraordinary Why Companion Workbook.* Its exercises and additional content are designed to help you gain the most from our experience together. Doing either will ensure you glean maximum value from your investment of time.

What we do in life echoes in eternity!

Now that you've gotten a taste of the power of drama, let's dive into another movie!

In *Gladiator,*[iii] the five-time Academy Award-Winning film including Best Picture of 2000, we meet the great Roman Emperor Marcus Aurelius and his faithful general, Maximus Decimus Meridius, Commander of the Armies of the North, General of the Felix Legions.

In the opening scene, Maximus, brilliantly portrayed by Russell Crowe, rallies his troops for the final battle against the barbarian, Germanic tribes.

"Brothers!" Maximus shouts so that all the troops can hear him.

"What we do in life echoes in eternity!"

What we do in life <u>echoes</u> in eternity!

Turning to his Lieutenant General, Quintus, Maximus issues his order:

"Quintus, on my command, unleash hell."

Quintus unleashes that very hell! With Maximus' inspirational cry still ringing in their ears, the assembled Roman armies vanquish their final foe. After the battle, the Emperor's son, heir-apparent to the throne, Commodus, arrives late to the scene:

"Did I miss the battle father?" he inquires meekly, feigning actual concern as he stands amidst a battlefield filled with the wrecked bodies of brave heroic souls.

"You missed the war son," Aurelius replies dryly, with obvious, but not unexpected disappointment in his tone. *"But fear not ... Maximus handled it for us,"* he concludes revealing his unveiled pride in the general he wishes he could call 'son' as well.

Early the next morning, Aurelius, wonderfully played by Richard Harris, summons Maximus to his tent. Maximus arrives to find his old, tired emperor, a man he loves like a father, working hard at his papers by dim candlelight. Clearly, Aurelius is occupied with his thoughts. Standing at full attention just inside the tent's entrance, Maximus announces his arrival. Without looking up, Aurelius responds:

"Tell me again Maximus." Long pause, then: *"WHY are we here?"*

Taken aback by the question, Maximus, nonetheless, quickly replies:

"For the glory of The Empire, Caesar! For Rome!"

Then, in this intense scene, Aurelius breaks down the barriers of status between Emperor and mere subject. He invites Maximus to dispense with the formalities, take a seat, and join him in simple conversation. Maximus sits, and Aurelius continues:

"I am dying Maximus. I'm dying. When a man sees his end, he wants to know his life had some kind of meaning, purpose. How will the world speak my name? Will I be known as 'The Philosopher?' 'The Warrior?' 'The Tyrant?'" he adds as a final possibility raising a skeptical eyebrow of concern at the thought of 'Tyrant' being his ultimate legacy.

But then, he continues more hopefully:

"Or will I be the Emperor who gave Rome back her true self? There was once a dream that was Rome! You could only whisper it – anything more than a whisper, and it would vanish. It was so fragile ... and I fear it will not survive winter. Come, my friend, let us whisper now, together, you and I."

In the whispering that takes place, Aurelius confides he knows his son Commodus is neither moral nor fit to lead the Empire. That he would lead only for selfish gain.

So, Aurelius challenges Maximus to succeed him as Caesar – to rid The Senate of its political corruption and to return Rome back to the people making her a Republic once more.

"Will you accept this great honor that I offer you?"

"With all my heart, no Sire!" Maximus faithfully responds, horrified at the thought of losing his beloved King.

"That is why it must be you, Maximus. Will you do this for me? The dying wish of an old man, and friend?"

"I need some time, Sire."

"Of course. Now embrace me as my son and bring an old man another blanket."

It's a beautiful, touching scene. Resplendently acted, superbly directed. Even the hardest heart of the toughest viewer is moved. Why? Because we connect with our own mortality – our own parents, children, legacy.

The problem, of course, arises when Aurelius breaks the news to his boy. Commodus does NOT take it well. Aurelius tries to console him. He kneels before Commodus and bids his son to embrace him.

Commodus does just that. Hugging him to his breast WAY too tightly, suffocating him.

Commodus kills his father.

Then he commands Quintus to kill Maximus. Quintus fails in the attempt but wounds Maximus quite badly. Commodus orders Maximus' wife and son to be killed. Maximus becomes enslaved.

Maximus becomes … 'Gladiator.'

NOW: We have the setting for a powerful drama!

We *know* how this drama will end: with these two men, Maximus and Commodus, face-to-face in the Roman Coliseum.

We just don't know how we're going to get there. That's the drama. That's what sucks us in – gets us onto the edge of the seat, wanting more.

Let us whisper together

That's also my invitation to you as you read this book:

> *Let us whisper now together you and I.*
> *About your legacy.*
> *About how you'll be remembered after you're gone.*

It's an invitation to make your life *extraordinary!*

I'm *not* inviting you to reflect upon 'which buildings at which universities will bear your name' after your passing. I'm not talking about *Ego Management*. It's deeper than that. Nor is this an exercise in people pleasing. It's not our job to be 'liked' by people. It's our duty to deal *righteously* with people. Whether they like it or not is irrelevant. We're not talking about such superficialities.

Instead, this is an exercise in prioritization. This is an invitation for you to consider where you're investing your only limited resource – *your time.*

On this journey, you'll encounter people, projects, and relationships that matter deeply to you. You'll find out *why* they matter so much to you. You'll commit to invest more of the time you have left into those priorities. You'll also have an opportunity to spend some quality time with your *Conscience* – your guide, who will illuminate your *Extraordinary Why* – your *purpose*.

It is in fulfilling your Extraordinary Why that you'll discover a life of significance that truly matters!

Not a journey for the faint of heart

Before you agree to travel with me, however, let me warn you: This is *not* a journey for the faint of heart. Sometimes along the way, you may encounter one or more of the following:

- Broken relationships in your past or present
- People who have hurt you or people you have hurt
- Projects that matter but you've abandoned
- Harbored grudges or bitterness from an unforgiven offense
- An unhealed wound of some kind

When we encounter such things, feelings, and relationships, it can get emotional, uncomfortable.

I understand!

But, I lead you on this journey for the following reason:

> While it's possible to grow and improve while remaining *comfortable*, if you want a *breakthrough* – if you want to *lead* and *be* at a higher level than ever before, there's only one way to achieve that level of *transformative* growth.

You have to journey right to the very edge of your comfort zone – to the very frontier of where you've traveled before but have turned back in the past. When you get to *that* place, you must bravely and boldly continue forward. You must embrace the discomfort and press on through it.

> *Transformation <u>only</u> takes place*
> *<u>outside</u> our comfort zone.*

Winston Churchill once said: "If you ever find yourself going through hell ... keep on going!"

In my decade of coaching CEOs and leaders of businesses, not-for-profits, civic associations and church leaders – coaching them to, and through, breakthrough transformation – here's what I've learned:

> *What we each want most out of life*
> *lies on the other side*
> *of what we fear most greatly.*

Are you willing to travel with me on this journey?

To give yourself permission to be emotional?

To acknowledge and confront your fears?

To embrace discomforts and bravely move forward through them?

If so, with your conscience alongside you as your guide, I promise this will be a transformative, life-changing experience for you.

I certainly understand why you might not want to come along on this journey. Who wants to be *un*comfortable? So, *'I'm not sure'* and *'No way'* are perfectly acceptable answers.

Most people take that safer path. It's far more comfortable!

If that's where you are at the moment, don't rush it. Set the book down for a while. Go for a walk, a hike, a swim. Ponder the possibility over time. When you sense you might be ready to reconsider your answer, pick the book back up.

Return to this place. This fork in the road:

Two roads diverged in a wood, and I —
I took the one less traveled by,
And that has made all the difference.
— Robert Frost

Personally, I think 'Yes' is the better answer.

Carpe diem! Seize the day!

But the choice, of course, is completely yours.

Are you up for the journey?

Think it through. Turn to the next chapter only when you're sure you're all in!

"When a man sees his end,
he wants to know his life
had some kind of meaning. Purpose."
— Marcus Aurelius (in Gladiator)

NOTES

i. *Dead Poet's Society,* directed by Peter Weir (1989; Los Angeles, CA: Touchstone Pictures, 1998), DVD.

ii. "Carpe Diem – Seize the Day." *Dead Poet's Society,* directed by Peter Weir (1989; Los Angeles, CA: Touchstone Pictures, 1998), DVD.

iii. *Gladiator,* directed by Ridley Scott. (2000; Los Angeles, CA: Universal Pictures, 2000), DVD.

Chapter 2

Your Guidance System

*"The only tyrant I accept in this world is
the 'still small voice' within me."*
— Ghandi

"It is neither right nor safe to go against my conscience."
— Martin Luther

*"The voice of conscience is so delicate it's easy to stifle;
so clear it's impossible to mistake."*
— Anne Germain De Stael

Goals, Destinations and Compass Headings

In what is perhaps the greatest personal development book of the
20th Century, *Seven Habits of Highly Effective People,*[i] Stephen Covey
presents a powerful life habit: *'Begin with the End in Mind.'*

Introducing that habit to his readers, Covey takes them on a
visualization trip. It's a journey of the imagination – similar to our
April 1888 trip to Paris, France. Covey asks readers to envision their
own funeral.

If you're following along in the *Extraordinary Why Companion Workbook*,
you can complete this similar exercise *(now would be a great time to do so!).*

It's a time in the near future. You've passed. A ceremony is held to honor you and the life you chose to live. Speakers from your family, your workplace, your friend groups, and your community give eulogies, capturing the essence of who you were – the impact you had.

After visualizing the experience, you write down what you'd like each speaker to be able to say about you and the life you chose to live. It's a provocative experience that brings you face-to-face with your own mortality – your most deeply held values. The exercise ensures you make contact with your conscience.

Why would Covey use that exercise to introduce a habit he calls:

'Begin with the End in Mind'?

Let's start with the obvious connection:

First, your funeral marks your *end* – your literal end. That moment when the *physical* portion of your reality comes to a screeching halt, and that next phase of your existence begins – whatever that may be for you.

By going to that end and writing down the words you'd like your closest friends and family to say, you've actually set goals, haven't you? Goals. Specific 'destinations' at which you one-day hope to arrive.

Because these goals were made after establishing contact with one's conscience, people often refer to them as *compass* headings.

THIS is 'True North' for me. THIS, specifically, is what I want this person to be able to say about who I was to them while I lived. It's my guiding compass!

Occasionally, someone suggests this exercise provides a 'Roadmap' for life ahead. But that's not quite right, is it? There's a difference between a Goal, a Destination, a Compass Heading, and a Roadmap, isn't there?

Let's return to the world of film to consider the possibility:

In the 2012 Spielberg movie *Lincoln*,[ii] Daniel Day Lewis wins an Oscar for his portrayal of the title role. He's superb. If you enjoy historical dramas, period pieces, you must see this film.

It's been reported that during the entire filming, Lewis never came out of character – even off set – which must have been really weird for his family!

In Lewis' acceptance speech for the Best Actor Oscar, he thanked his wife for her *'willingness to live with so many different men'* during the course of their relationship! That's how he does it! It's his 'secret sauce.' He completely immerses himself in his roles and literally becomes the character.

The method obviously works for him because he's the only actor in history to win that coveted award three times: (*Lincoln* (2012), *My Left Foot: The Story of Christy Brown* (1990), and *There Will be Blood* (2007)), and he's been nominated for three others - wow!

In the scene I'll describe for you, Lincoln sits across a dimly lit dinner table from a lesser-known character in American History – Thaddeus Stevens.

Stevens was an abolitionist staunchly committed to a specific worthy goal of his own. He was committed the pursuit of passing the 13th Amendment to the US Constitution, thereby abolishing slavery in the United States. He's undeniably passionate about the cause. Throughout the film, Stevens berates Lincoln for not leading more effectively to that end.

Stevens, expertly played by Tommy Lee Jones, lets Lincoln have it:

*"I don't [care] what the people want ... the people elected me to represent them, to lead them and I lead. You ought to try it! You claim you trust 'em, but you KNOW what the people are. You know that the inner **compass** that should direct the soul toward justice has ossified in white men and women – North and South – unto utter uselessness through tolerating the evil of slavery."*

Lincoln pauses briefly to reflect on what's just been said. Then he adds his own thoughts to the conversation:

"A compass, I learned when I was surveying, it'll point you True North from where you're standing. But it's got no advice about the swamps, deserts and chasms you'll encounter along the way. If in pursuit of your destination you plunge ahead heedless of obstacles and achieve nothing more than to sink in a swamp ... what's the use in knowing True North?"

Lincoln makes a great point: It's good to have a destination in mind and a compass pointing us toward our initial direction. Yet, a compass is oblivious to the obstacles between our intended destination and where we are today.

We need something even more valuable than a compass.

We need a *guidance system.*

Only our *'conscience'* informs us if we're making progress toward our intended destinations or even if those desired destinations are the right ones to pursue in the first place!

If you really *were* to travel to Paris, France, you likely wouldn't head out in the direction you initially pointed at the beginning of this book.

Rather, you'd probably make your way to the nearest international airport and board a plane. Otherwise, you'd never clear any of those obstacles (oceans, canyons, border crossings) between where you are at the moment and that romantic City of Lights.

A compass is valuable for sure. But it must be calibrated by *your conscience* – your guidance system.

Your Guidance System

Consider a guided missile in flight. What percentage of time is it heading perfectly towards its intended target with exactly the right pitch, roll, yaw and attitude? Any guesses?

When I ask my audiences that question, invariably, the quickest answer is usually something like: "Less than 1%." To which I quickly reply: "Less than 1%? That's like a North Korean missile. *We've launched it, but we have NO CLUE where it's going, so look out!'* It's a very unpredictable and dangerous weapon!"

That's usually followed by some loud, nervous, laughter.

Kidding aside that low number probably isn't all that far off. The actual number varies, of course, but some estimates are as low as 6%. Imagine that! Just 6% perfectly on-target, which frighteningly means that 94% of the time, it's off course!

Onboard gyroscopes regularly adjust to feedback received from accelerometers. They spin to shift the missile's pitch, roll, and yaw, altering the missile's *attitude*[iii] as it travels. 94% of the time, it is off-course, yet with constant adjustments, it manages to reach its intended target. Interesting.

Have you ever been on an airplane when right before landing, the pilot makes a major change of course or direction, perhaps adjusting to a big gust of wind? Or worse yet, you're just about to touch down on the runway when the pilot hits the thrusters urgently and you take back off? Ever have an aborted landing like that?

"Whoa!" you exclaim, tensing up. "What's going on?"

Big corrections, right before landing, are never good. They can result in an 'unplanned landing' – a 'crash!'

Conversely, small corrections, farther away from the runway, are imperceptible to passengers aboard. You touch down perfectly at your intended destination, even though you've been off-course some large percentage of time.

Where's the connection for us? How do we make similar *life* corrections? We're not planes or guided missiles. We don't have "pitch," "roll," "yaw" or "attitude." Do we?

Well, we DO have "attitude!"

at ˈti ˈtude

[ˈadə‚t(y)o͞od]

NOUN

- the orientation of an aircraft or spacecraft, relative to the direction of travel...

    AND

- a settled way of thinking or feeling about someone or something, typically one that is reflected in a person's behavior.

As humans, we have *'attitudes, behaviors, choices, and decisions.'* These are the As, Bs, Cs, & Ds (*ABCDs*), the vectors we adjust as we travel on our journey towards the targets, the goals, we've committed to accomplish.

Take a look at the following picture show in figure 2.1:

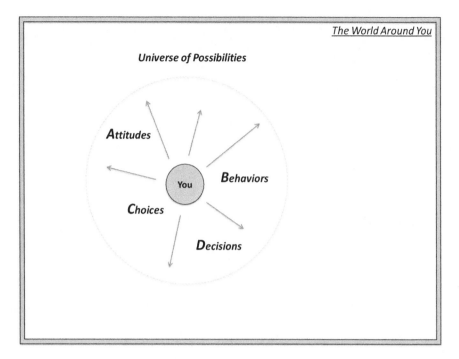

Figure 2.1

Around you, at any moment, in any set of circumstances, there is a universe of possible attitudes, behaviors, choices, and decisions at your disposal. Some may be significant while others may be less consequential. Regardless of the size or magnitude, each will move you from where you are at the present moment to some other place.

Your attitudes, behaviors, choices, and decisions *(Your ABCDs)* might move you *physically* from one locale to another: from the couch to the gym, or from Los Angeles to Paris, for example.

Your *ABCDs* might move you *intellectually*: from ignorance to knowledge, or from novice and inexperienced to capable and skilled. They might move you *emotionally* from one mood to another: from calm and peaceful to irritated and angry or from melancholy and blasé to inspired and engaged.

Still again, your *ABCDs* could move you *spiritually*: from disconnected, fearful and isolated to centered, worshipful, and whole.

Even the choice to 'do nothing' and remain stationary, for example, moves you because we don't operate in a vacuum. We live and operate in a frame of reference. The world around you is constantly changing. So, even if you *choose* to 'do nothing' and remain still in your present position, the world around you shifts relative to you. So, in fact, you have *moved* relative to the world even by remaining stationary.

There really is no escaping the fact that *your attitudes, behaviors, choices, and decisions make you a powerful being.*

Calibrating your Guidance System

Your *ABCDs* affect not only you, but also others around you. Think about it this way:

The world around you is influenced, for better or for worse, by:

- the **attitudes you display,**
- the **behaviors you demonstrate,**
- the **choices you consider**, and
- the **decisions you make** in each moment.

Pause for a few moments to consider what it means *to you.*

That phrase, *'for better or for worse,'* is an interesting one to ponder, isn't it? It presupposes a *value system* of some kind. Establishing contact with your conscience connects you with *your own personal value system.* Regular contact with your value system is crucial to ensure that your compass remains well-calibrated.

> *When your ABCDs and your personal value system are aligned, you have Integrity of Being.*

That's an incredibly freeing experience that only a regularly consulted relationship with a well-calibrated compass can provide!

In their outstanding book *Accelerate – High Leverage Leadership for Today's World"*, my good friends Suzanne Mayo Frindt and Dwight Frindt introduce a paradigm called *Vision-Focused Leadership.*^{TM} They define it, essentially, as leading from a mental model of some desired future state. When used effectively, it has catalyzing power to transform an organization.

A key element of *Vision-Focused Leadership*^{TM} is a concept they call the *Yonder Star.* In their words:

> *"The Yonder Star is the ideal, out in front of you and up above the path you are currently traveling, that provides a common focus and inspires your actions. Priorities, plans, and milestones are designed from a focus on the Yonder Star. From this mindset, actions are prioritized by their value in fulfilling the Yonder Star."*

Suzanne and Dwight model this kind of leadership in the very name of their company, 2130 Partners. That name, and their core philosophy, is derived from a Native American insight (often attributed to the Iroquois Confederacy). The premise is this:

"Leaders are accountable in their decision-making for their impact on each of the next seven generations."

The Frindts founded their business in 1990. Seven generations of twenty years each makes 140 years. Dwight and Suzanne lead their company from a commitment to work from that long-term, *Yonder Star*, vision they're striving to achieve out in the year 2130.

Talk about a long-term vision … a Yonder Star, indeed!

I love this model and way of thinking for a business and an organization. Think of the power that's unleashed when everyone in an organization shares a common vision of the world around them 140 years out into the future!

It works well for an individual life and legacy too!

Remember, your legacy is not you. It doesn't even belong to you –
your legacy belongs to others. You can certainly influence it, but it's
separate from *you*. It's how others will remember you – how they'll
speak of you after you're gone. Your legacy doesn't exist in the
present. It exists in another person's heart and mind, in the future,
after you're gone.

With that in mind, take a look at this diagram:

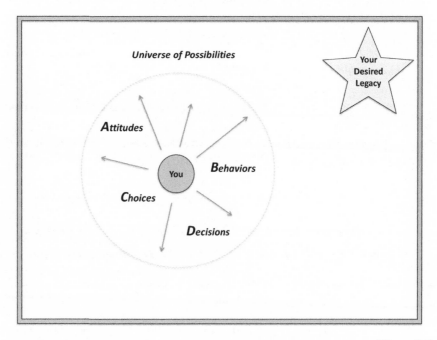

Figure 2.2

In Figure 2.2, notice the addition of *'Your Desired Legacy.'* It's shown as
a *'Yonder Star'* – *'out in front of you, up above your current path'*

In any given circumstance, a universe of possible attitudes,
behaviors, choices, and decisions surrounds you. Some will lead you
closer to fulfilling the legacy that matters most to you. Others will take
you further away from your desired legacy.

A defined *'Desired Legacy'* provides a focal point. It inspires future *ABCDs*, leading to its fulfillment. But any pilot or astronaut can tell you: navigating towards a single point without a frame of reference is impossible.

While your *ABCDs* are constantly moving you, don't miss this: *other people are moving too – because of their own ABCDs and also in response to your ABCDs.* Navigating in such a dynamic environment is impossible without a defined frame of reference.

Thankfully, when it comes to this thing called life, we have one!

I'll bring it to life with a quick story:

In college, I was not a very good student. I attended engineering school at the University of Virginia, distinguishing myself by making the Dean's List. Not the one I wanted to be on, however. No, I made the Dean's List of *Students on Academic Probation.* Not just once but *twice*! It took me five years to graduate. I finally earned my Engineering Degree – on the promise that I'd pursue a career in Business, lest I do lasting harm to human life and physical infrastructure!

One thing I did learn though was that when plotting a graph, there's always a horizontal X-axis and a vertical Y-axis.

In life, your X-axis is *Time.* It's constantly marching forward. You cannot control it. *Time* is 'independent' of you. It defines the one steady dimension of your operating frame of reference.

'Negative' *Time* is everything in your past, to the left on your timeline.

'Positive' *Time* is everything in your future, to the right on your timeline.

For the purposes of navigating and living an extraordinary life that leads to *Your Yonder Star – Desired Legacy*, your Y-axis is your *State of Being* relative to your *Value System.*

'Negative' *States of Being* are *ABCDs* that lead you farther away from *Your Desired Legacy*.

'Positive' *States of Being* are *ABCDs* that lead you closer to *Your Desired Legacy*.

I've added that operating frame of reference to Figure 2.3 below:

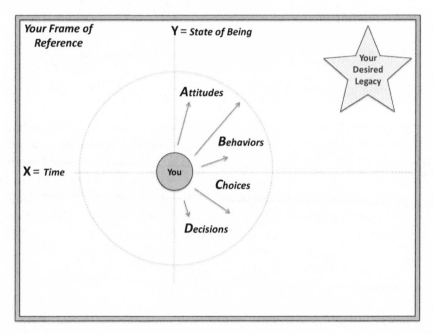

Figure 2.3

With a defined operating frame of reference, effective navigation is now possible. How does that work?

Well, often your previous attitude, behavior, choice, or decision to a given circumstance *informs* your next *ABCD* when a similar circumstance arises. You acted one way in the past, making it easier to act the same way in the future. *ABCDs* tend to build on and reinforce each other.

Over time, you create *Habits* through this repetitive, learned process of reinforcement.

Habits can be:

- Unintentional, reflexive *attitudes*
- Patterns of *behavior*
- A limited view of the *choices* available to you
- Knee-jerk *decisions* in the form of *triggered reactions* to circumstances vs. *considered responses*

Positive habits create *positive momentum* toward *Your Desired Legacy*. Negative habits create *negative momentum* away from *Your Desired Legacy*. While you can't change your past, with this *Frame of Reference* in place, you can now focus attention on your future *ABCDs* – those you can still control, to the right of you on your timeline.

This additional information is shown below in Figure 2.4:

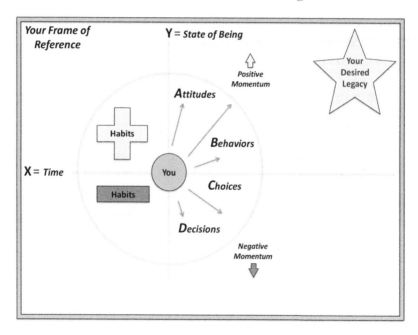

Figure 2.4

In your future, there are 90 degrees (upper right quadrant) of *attitudes*, *behaviors, choices,* and *decisions* that lead you closer to the legacy you truly want to leave in the lives of those that matter most to you. When you operate and live in that space, you generate even more positive momentum and move powerfully towards *Your Desired Legacy*.

Sadly, there are also 90 degrees (lower right quadrant) of future *ABCDs* that lead you farther away from leaving that legacy. Living and operating in that space generates negative momentum and hinders you from leaving behind the legacy that you'll find deeply satisfying in your final hours.

Most people are really good at working in the 90 degrees that take them closer to accomplishing the goals they want to achieve in business and life. That's *why and how* they get things done. They set a goal, and from the day they do, they constantly adapt to whatever circumstances come their way. They adjust, change, and maneuver until they make forward progress. Eventually, this enables them to achieve what they set out to do (and get those euphoric feelings from doing so)!

It's a rare person who gives ample thought or attention to those things that can lead them away from their intended goals – those *ABCDs* that take them farther away from being who they really want to be. But, perhaps a bit of attention to those things is called for?

That remarkable business icon, "The Oracle of Omaha," Warren Buffett once said:

> **"It takes 20 years to build a reputation –
> just five minutes to ruin it.**
>
> **If you think about that, you'll do things differently.""**

It's probably, therefore, worth spending just a few minutes considering some of the things that reside in the negative 90 degrees. Then, you can avoid being possessed by those *attitudes*. You can avoid *behaving* in ways hinder your progress. You can avoid considering *choices* and making *decisions* that hold you back from leaving the legacy you truly desire.

The Right Stuff and the Wrong Stuff

Those negatives are best summarized in the deeply spiritual prayer known as *'The Shepard's Prayer.'* Have you heard of this prayer?

You may think I'm speaking of that great passage from the 23rd Psalm? One of the many written by King David of Israel – arguably the most famous shepherd of all time. An understandable mistake since David certainly did a great deal of praying! You know *that* particular passage:

"The Lord is my *shepherd*, I shall not want ..."

But, that's *not* 'The Shepard's Prayer' to which I'm referring. No, the one I'm thinking of was made famous in yet another movie!

This prayer was uttered by one of the main characters in the 1983 Film, *The Right Stuff* – winner of four Academy Awards for its technical achievements and nominated for a Best Picture Oscar. This adaptation of Tom Wolfe's bestseller appeared on almost every "Top Ten" Best Picture list for the year. It featured an all-star cast including Scott Glenn who portrayed the character that muttered this, not-so-proverbial, prayer.

Let me set the stage:

The film begins by introducing us to the many brave, mostly nameless, American test pilots back in the late, post-WWII 1940s. They were attempting to break the Sound Barrier of Mach 1.0. The movie continues to follow them through the 1950s and 60s and gives us a front row seat into what ultimately became the Great Space Race between the Americans and the Russians.

America was frantically trying to beat the Soviets into outer space, yet Explorer I feebly sits on the ground as the Russians successfully launch Sputnik into space from Star City, Russia on October 4th, 1957, becoming the first nation to escape Earth's gravitational pull.

Ever optimistic, the USA redoubles its efforts, committed to winning the big prize – being first to get a man into space. Failures ensue. Rockets explode. Countdowns begin – missions are scrubbed. Often, an elderly, shadowy character, clearly representing *Death,* watches on as the astronauts' frustrations build to a crescendo.

Finally, in the early dawn moments of May 5th, 1961, the American astronaut, Alan B. Shepard, boldly approaches the, essentially untested, Mercury-Redstone 3 rocket named *Freedom 7*. It had never been used to launch a human before.

Before he ascends to the top of the rocket, Shepard looks *Death* squarely in the eye before breaking the glance and turning to the mission before him. *Death*, grimly, almost reluctantly, watches our hero until he disappears into the elevator that will hoist him to what could be his final resting place.

What do we notice in *Death's* expression in this poignant moment? It doesn't appear to be the gleeful anticipation we might expect to see on *Death's* face. No. It's far more somber. Could it be 'dismay' we sense? Dread of the moment when he must announce yet another passing to a fearful and still unknowing new widow?

That question appears to be answered as Shepard disappears from view. We see *Death*, along with all the other smiling admirers, nodding and beginning to clap as the astronaut ascends the towering rocket. Clearly there's a degree of respect being shown here. Respect for a man willing to stare *Death* right in the face and proceed forward with the mission despite the risk.

Here is a man who's 'all-in.' "Bring it on!" appears to be his attitude, and even *Death* is visibly moved, impressed. Shepard climbs into the tiny capsule atop the massive structure. The hatch is closed and secured. Alone for the first time, he utters his prayer.

The 'deeply spiritual' prayer that will forever forth be known as the Shepard's Prayer:

"Dear Lord, please don't let me #@$! up."

Sorry! Clearly a PG13 rating, I'm afraid.

NOT the prayer I would have prayed!

"Lord! Don't let me die when they 'light this candle!'

That's what I would have prayed. Keep me alive! Please ... don't let me die! But for Shepard and every astronaut that's ever sat atop that rocket, here's the mindset:

I probably __will__ die when they light this candle. __That's__ the most likely outcome. But I'm here for a __purpose__. I'm here to get us into space. I'm here to set the program forward. I'm here to bring honor and glory to the Nation ... maybe my own family name in the process. Yet here I sit, in front of all these switches, levers, dials and knobs and if I do the wrong thing, at the wrong time, I could do the exact opposite of why I'm here. I could set the program years backwards. I could disgrace my nation – bring shame upon my family name. __When__ I die ... let me die well!

That prayer 'Don't let me *mess* up' has been voiced so many times in the capsule atop a rocket that it's now often called *The Astronaut's Prayer*.

Not exactly spiritual. But oh, so profound!

"Don't let me mess up. I've got __one shot__ at this ... please let me get it right!"

Shepard DID get it right. He clearly had the 'Right Stuff!' His attitudes, behaviors, choices, and decisions led him closer toward his desired legacy. Today, he is remembered as a true American Hero.

For dramatic purposes, the movie also provided a contrasting example.

The second American in space was Virgil Ivan (Gus) Grissom, who launched on July 21st, 1961. That mission didn't go as well as Shepard's. Grissom's capsule was lost at sea after it splashed down. In the film, Grissom is blamed for the failure. The film leads us to believe that Grissom packed his space suit with rolls of dimes and trinkets to offer for sale when he returned – presumably for personal profit.

When NASA discovered that Grissom had jeopardized the mission by carrying aboard extra weight, he was not hailed as a hero.

"I didn't do anything wrong!" Grissom angrily, vehemently protested.

The filmmakers lead us to believe that Grissom put his own self-interest above the best interest of the mission. Such attitudes, behaviors, choices, and decisions negatively impacted his *Yonder Star - Desired Legacy.*

Later in the film, over a meal with one of his fellow Mercury Seven Astronauts, Gordon Cooper, we see a quieter, calmer Grissom. The less-experienced Cooper receives advice from his friend. A more self-reflective Grissom finally owns his previous shortcoming. He turns to his friend and essentially says in a low, somber, mentoring-style voice:

"Hey Gordo … just make sure you don't mess up like I did."

BE *better than I was* – Be BETTER.

Sage advice indeed for us all. None of us is perfect. We all make mistakes. But, we can all also commit to 'be better than we were.' Not repeat the mistakes of our past as we journey forward in life toward the legacy we will ultimately leave behind.[vii]*

---

* Please read the end of chapter note for an expanded, more complete description of Gus Grissom's ultimate legacy.

In summary, this is the model we'll keep in front of us as we travel on our journey together:

There's a specific desired legacy you'd like to leave behind in the hearts and minds of people who matter most to you. In each circumstance you encounter, there are 90 degrees of future attitudes, behaviors, choices, and decisions that lead you closer to leaving that legacy behind. There are also 90 degrees of *ABCDs* that take you farther away from leaving that legacy.

Your *ABCDs* can **help** you or **hinder** you.

Without a guidance system – a closely cultivated, well-calibrated relationship with your *conscience* – you're like that proverbial North Korean Missile – you don't have a clue, which way you're traveling!

Where we're going on our journey

As you continue to read, please do so intentionally, reflectively.

Think of the time you invest in this material as a unique opportunity: *a chance to make fresh contact with your conscience (that still, small, voice you've known your whole life).*

I'm affording you the opportunity to calibrate your guidance system to ensure that it's steering you rightly – toward the legacy that you will find deeply satisfying in your final hours.

Elisabeth Kubler-Ross said it well:

> *"It is not the end of the physical body that should worry us.*
> *Rather our concern must be to **live while we're alive** –*
> *to release our inner selves from the spiritual death that comes with*
> *living behind a facade designed to conform to external definitions of*
> *who and what we are."*

What you get out of this experience will be proportionate to what you bring to it. I encourage you, again: follow along in the _Extraordinary Why Companion Workbook._ That way, on our journey together, when you find areas where you're on track, heading in the right direction, you can document those areas to ensure you stay the course. Should you happen to identify areas where your flight path needs adjustment, you can record course corrections you need to make.

That's what successful people of significance do with consistency: They regularly assess where they are vs. where they need to be. They make necessary adjustments to ensure they ultimately manage to hit their intended targets.

**Successful people of significance regularly assess where they are vs. where they need to be and make necessary adjustments.**

To recap our objectives as we travel on this journey together, this is an opportunity for you to:

- Identify the big _whys_ in your life, including _your Extraordinary Why_, your purpose,

AND ...

- Cultivate a deeper, more intimate relationship with your conscience, to calibrate your guidance system and ensure that it's steering you rightly.

Still on board for the ride? Terrific. Let's keep on going!

"Through pride we are ever deceiving ourselves.
But deep down below the surface of the average conscience
a still, small voice says to us, something is out of tune."
– Carl Jung

NOTES

i.   Stephen R. Covey, *7 Habits of Highly Effective People* (New York, NY: Simon & Schuster, 1989).

ii.   *Lincoln*, directed by Steven Spielberg (2012; Los Angeles, CA: Dreamworks/ Twentieth Century Fox, 2013), DVD.

iii.   In aviation and space flight, *attitude* provides information about an object's orientation with respect to the local level frame (horizontal plane) and *True North*. Global Navigation Satellite System (GNSS) is the standard generic term for satellite navigation systems that provide autonomous geo-spatial positioning with global coverage. GNSS attitude solutions typically consist of three components: pitch, roll and yaw.

iv.   Dwight Frindt and Suzanne Frindt. *Accelerate – High Leverage Leadership for Today's World* (2130 Partners, 2010).

v.   Tuttle, Brad. "Warren Buffet's Boring, Brilliant Wisdom." Time. March, 2010. Accessed October 28, 2019. http://business.time.com/2010/03/01/warren-buffetts-boring-brilliant-wisdom/

vi.   *The Right Stuff*, directed by Philip Kaufman (1983; Los Angeles, CA: The Ladd Company and Warner Brothers, 1997), DVD.

vii.   Before publishing this book, I had the privilege of having few conversations with a member of Gus Grissom's family. I learned that, from their perspective, Hollywood took quite a few liberties in telling Gus' story in *The Right Stuff*.

Apparently, Gus did take up two dimes with him on the flight … one for each of his sons. The family still cherishes both. This is a particularly interesting, and touching fact – especially in light of the much more modern movie *First Man*. That film chronicles the story of Neil Armstrong and the first Apollo moon landing. In case you haven't seen it, I won't spoil that film experience for you. Rather, I'll simply encourage you to watch it. The closing scene in *First Man* of Neil on the moon will most certainly bring the poignancy of Gus' choice to bring those dimes with him into space to life for you in a profound way! Ultimately, Grissom's legacy is not defined by this isolated, and overly exaggerated, event.

As a US Air Force pilot, Grissom flew over 100 missions during the Korean War and received the Air Medal with cluster and the Distinguished Flying Cross for his service. Four years after his controversial space flight as the second of the Mercury Seven astronauts, he was assigned another mission. Why would NASA grant him another mission if he lacked the character necessary to lead effectively?

On that mission, Gus commanded Gemini III, orbited Earth three times and safely returned to Earth with his co-pilot John Young. Both men were heralded as heroes upon their return and awarded the Distinguished Service Medal by President Lyndon B. Johnson.

Of particular significance, Grissom was selected to command the first manned mission of what would become known as Apollo 1. Tragically, Grissom and the rest of his crew, Ed White and Roger Chaffee, never made it into space. They died on January 27, 1967, in fire during a pre-flight test at the NASA Space Center in Cape Kennedy (now Cape Canaveral), Florida, a scene powerfully depicted in _First Man._

Gus left behind a wife and two children. In the immediate aftermath of the fire, NASA made several design changes to the Apollo spacecraft. His colleagues knew Grissom as the 'Engineer of Engineers.' He was the 'go-to guy' to solve tough problems. To this day, the agency still commemorates the anniversary of the Apollo 1 fire in late January with a moment of silence. Quite the tribute!

Grissom knew his work was dangerous, but important. In the book _Footprints on the Moon_ he's quoted:

> _"If we die, we want people to accept it. We're in a risky business, and we hope that if anything happens to us it will not delay the program. The conquest of space is worth the risk of life."_

I prefer to think that this quote sums up the life and legacy of Gus Grissom more accurately and completely than he was portrayed in _The Right Stuff._

Chapter 3

Your Personal Timeline

"There is nothing so wretched or foolish
as to anticipate misfortunes.
What madness it is in your expecting
evil before it arrives!"
— Seneca

Your 'End Date' – Why's that so difficult?

When are you going to die? Jarring question, isn't it?

Nonetheless, take a moment to consider the two years that will populate your headstone. Write them in the spaces below. *(Hint: the first one should be easy!)*

_____   _____
Born   *Died*

Now ... do the math:

How old will you be in that last year? _____

My Expected Age of Death

What's so hard about considering the year of your own death or the age at which you'll die? Most people find some degree of difficulty doing so. Why?

Here are the main reasons I hear from people all over the world:

1) *"I just don't like thinking about my passing."* Most of us like thinking we will go on forever. We prefer to fantasize that our timeline here on Earth is 'a ray' that goes on continuously. Not a 'line segment.' Certainly not a short one! No matter how definite our ultimate demise may be, most of us just don't like dwelling upon it.

2) *"The subject of death is 'taboo' – off limits."* I've delivered my workshops to tens of thousands of people, in hundreds of groups, in numerous cultures, on six of the seven continents around the world. I've yet to encounter a group that doesn't have some degree of internal angst when I ask them to contemplate their own demise. Most people avoid this kind of contemplation. They find it morbid, morose – even *creepy*.

3) *"Personal pain often seems to accompany dying."* Sometimes, thinking about *the process of dying* is even worse than the thought of being dead. Many of us have lost loved ones. We've watched them pass with great difficulty – slow, even agonizing deaths. Such experiences can make even the most faithful among us shrink back from confronting our own entrance to 'the glory that awaits.' We may truly want to get to heaven; we just don't want to die to get there!

4) *"Death involves sorrow & suffering for those we leave behind."* Nearly everyone has experienced sorrow and discomfort following the loss of a loved one. The very thought of those *we* love being sad because of our own passing is uncomfortable.

While it would be nice to have lived in such a way that those we've left behind miss us and wish we were still around, ultimately we don't want them to suffer – at least not for long. Thinking of our death makes us confront this painful reality: *the suffering of those we hold most dear.*

5) *"I'm not writing <u>anything</u> into that final blank!"* Be honest: Did you have a moment of pause when I asked you to consider the year of your own death? Perhaps you still haven't written anything into that second space? What's that all about? Some might call it 'superstitious' – but there's more to it than that. It's tied into a powerful reality.

Everything that exists in physical reality was created twice. Consider your cellphone. It's a real physical object – it exists. Yes? Mine is an iPhone. It was created twice. The first creation was in Steve Jobs' mind. First, he conceived it:

> *'The people don't know what they want. They don't have a clue! I will invent it and then they will want it!'*

Steve was a true innovator. After envisioning his goal and devising his plan, he probably wrote it down and described it. He even dared to speak it aloud. Subsequently, the capable people at Apple in Cupertino, CA got to work, and only then did it finally come into physical being. That's the creative process:

First, we think it. Then, we speak it.
Then, it comes into physical reality!

We know this to be true. So, sometimes our pre-conditioned reaction at a subconscious level to the question of, *"When are you going to die?"* is an immediate 'freeze' reaction:

> *'I'm NOT even going to entertain that question!'*

We are powerful beings, created in the image of our Creator who *spoke* the world into existence 'out of nothing' *(ex nihilo)*. We, too, therefore have the power to create. Not 'out of nothing,' of course, but we do have the power to build up with the words that we speak. We also have the power to destroy and tear down. This is not a power to be taken lightly.

For example, let's say, in reality, you were destined to live to 82, but you just considered '78' in response to that opening question. Did you just cheat yourself out of 4 years of life by creating that reality in your mind? Yikes! Not the point of the exercise, but certainly a valid reason for not wanting to 'go there!'

6) *"How we feel about this end-of-life exercise is often a function of where we currently are on the timeline."* A 20-year-old often approaches this activity very differently than a 70-year-old, for obvious reasons! While we're on this point, where are you currently on your timeline? 1ˢᵗ quarter? 1ˢᵗ half? 2ⁿᵈ half? Last quarter?

Your Past, Present, and Future

Think a bit more deeply about your current position on your timeline. Everything you've already experienced, of course, is called: *'Your Past.'* What can you do about it?

If your first thought is 'nothing,' you're not alone. That's almost always the first answer to that question. But, now think a bit deeper: What *can* you do about your past?

How about *learn* from it? Use your past experiences to *learn from them* – use your *past* to inform, advise, and *better* your future!

"These attitudes, behaviors, choices, and decisions (ABCDs) didn't work so well for me in the past. I think I'll do less of those in the days ahead! On the other hand, these other ABCDs actually turned our pretty well! I think I'll incorporate more of those into the time I have remaining!"

Good choices!

It's an exercise in futility to look back on our past and lament it, wishing it were different. It's a fool's errand to gaze back on our prior days of glory and revel in the 'good ol' times.' Why waste time in either of those ways?

That said, glances back into our history *can* be incredibly useful to us. If we travel down 'Memory Lane' intent on learning from our past, we can better ourselves by reconsidering our experiences in light of what we now know in the present. This is the 'calibration' process.

To the right side of your timeline resides everything you have yet to experience. It's called *'Your Future.'* Tomorrow and all the possibilities and opportunities it holds. All that potential out there, just waiting to be created by you! Exciting to consider it that way.

Of course, your current position on your timeline is called *'Your Present.'* Why?

Because *it's a gift!* Eleanor Roosevelt once famously said:

> *"Yesterday is history.*
> *Tomorrow is a mystery.*
> *But today is a gift — we're not promised another one.*
> *This is why we call it 'the present!'"*

The present! This moment. It *really* is a gift. It's precious!

It also happens to be the only place in which we're powerful. Think about it. Right now, in this moment, do you have any stress, worry, panic or anxiety?

Be honest. Is anything at all looming over you? For most of us, if we're completely honest with ourselves, the answer to that question is usually 'yes.'

This is the usual sentiment for a whole host of reasons:

- Job / career uncertainty
- Strained relationship(s) with our loved ones
- Financial concerns
- Car, house, or other maintenance nuisances
- Health issues of our own or with our loved ones
- Aging parents
- Kids going in wrong directions
- Etc., etc., etc!

All of these are, of course, valid reasons for concern. But when we allow our fears of the future to cause us stress, panic, or anxiety in the present, what we often fail to recognize is that we are making a choice to allow that to happen.

Unhealthy stress, anxiety or panic is tantamount to doing this: *Mentally accelerating negative future outcomes into our present moment.* Those things don't actually exist here and now, in our present, unless we *choose* to bring them. It's a *choice* to do so. The moment we make the choice to dwell on those negative outcomes, we render ourselves less powerful. Why? Because we become pre-occupied with things that, most likely, will never happen.

Choosing to focus on fear, panic, stress or anxiety is almost always a choice – a poor one at that. When we operate from such negative states of being we tend to *react* to circumstances. Triggered 'reactions' rarely yield positive outcomes.

Here's a better choice – take a deep breath and tell yourself:

> *"Whatever shows up in my future,*
> *I'm sure I'll be able to respond to it appropriately.*
> *So, I'm going to choose to leave it there."*

That choice makes you *powerful.* You freely choose the most useful attitude, behavior, choice, or decision in the present moment, leading you to the most favorable outcome in your future.

Sometimes, I get pushback on this point from detail-oriented *'planners'* in my audiences. You know, the CPAs, Insurance Agents, Bankers, Auditors and other risk-management specialists in the room. Gotta love 'em! Perhaps you're one of them? If so, "Thanks!" You often keep the rest of us out of a lot of trouble!

So, let me clarify: I'm all for that. Be intentional. Take some time occasionally to mentally envision your future and consider some of the negative outcomes that could befall you should you not be more prudent or thoughtful today. Then it's wise to make plans to reduce the risk of those things actually occurring. Once those plans are in place, return to the present moment.

Now you can have faith in your plans __and__ in your ability to respond appropriately to whatever shows up next.

This proactive practice enables you to be *fully present* in the current moment. There, in that space, you are powerful – capable of responding effectively as you consider and choose the most appropriate next step that's best for you and your loved ones.

Time & Death, Love & Beauty

With all the negativity associated with envisioning our timeline and our own demise, why do this?

Because:

Death gives Time its value!

Think about that for a moment.

Without death, time is worthless: 'I don't have to do anything with urgency — I have all the time in the world!'

Introduce *Death* into the equation *(and it IS part of the equation!),* and, instantly, *time becomes priceless!* **_Because_** of *Death, Time is _priceless!_*

The reality is this: we are a vapor, a mist, which is here today and gone tomorrow.[i] This singular, universal reality spurs the wise person into action!

What will __you__ do with the time that's left?

GREAT question! It will be the focus of our attention throughout our journey together.

Incidentally, *"Death gives time its value"* also happens to be yet another movie quote. I can't help myself! That line was featured in a marvelous film called _Collateral Beauty_[ii] starring Will Smith.

Do yourself a favor: Get together with a loved one, grab a box of tissues, perhaps a glass of wine, and watch the movie _Collateral Beauty_. It's the perfect 'Date Night' film. Or, watch it alone if you prefer.

In one of the opening scenes, Will Smith's character, Howard, specifically asks his large group of advertising agency employees:

"What is your __Why__? Your __Big Why__?"

Howard goes on to assert:

"We are here to connect. Life is about people ... and Love, Time and Death, these three abstractions connect every single human being on earth ... because, at the end of the day:

We long for love.
We wish we had more time.
We fear death."

When you watch the movie closely, you'll notice something wonderful: Those three characters, *Love, Time, and Death* are present in every scene of the movie from beginning to end. They are either physically present as actual characters in the scene, or they are present somehow in the background of *every* scene. It's fascinating to watch how the writer and director artfully achieve this feat throughout the film.

The same is, of course, true for us in real life: Love, Time and Death are omnipresent!

Love: She's *always* present around us. We may not always be aware of her presence, yet she's never distant. No further than a single attitude, behavior, choice, or decision *(ABCD)* away in every single moment of our lives.

In this next moment:

- Will I insist on my own way now or will I be patient?
- Will I judge or will I be kind?
- Will I envy my neighbor or remain content with my current lot?
- Will I be boastful and proud or will I be humble?
- Will I be brash and take what I want or will I give freely?
- Will I lash out in anger or will I control myself?
- Will I keep a running tally of the wrongs done to me or will I forgive others and seek forgiveness for the wrongs I've done?
- Will I delight when misfortune befalls my enemies or will I pray blessings for them?

- Will I rationalize wrong as right or will I rejoice that I know the difference and can stand for Truth?
- Will I abandon or protect? Be skeptical or trust? Despair of or hope for? Quit or persevere?

Love[iii] is always in our present if we choose to make her so in the moment.

Yet the moments are fleeting, because ...

Time is marching on ... always. Its rhythm: constant ... unrelenting. Time marks our years, months, weeks, days, hours, minutes and seconds.

If you have lived to a certain age, you know that, strangely, time seems to accelerate as we advance towards our inevitable conclusion.

Which, of course brings us to ...

Death: The specter of physical death is present all around us all the time. She looms in our future. We know she is there, but often we deny her existence as to do otherwise would be unnecessarily emotional, uncomfortable, and awkward. But we are indeed a mist, a vapor – here today, gone tomorrow. Physical death is our inevitable conclusion.

Ultimately, we all will meet with her ... personally. All too soon, if we're willing to be perfectly honest with ourselves.

Yes, *love, time and death* are ever-present. Here's the good news:

> You get to *choose* what to look for. You get to *choose* where to focus your attention!

What are your eyes set upon?

Are you noticing the <u>beauty</u> around you?

Beauty can also be found in every moment as well. Yet, if our gaze is set too low, on *Death* or *Time* for example, we can easily miss *Beauty*. *Beauty* can be the most illusive of all our present realities. Hence, the sage advice from Death's character in <u>*Collateral Beauty*</u>:

> *"... Just be sure to notice the collateral beauty along the way."*

In the film, the great British actress, Dame Helen Mirren, wonderfully portrays the character of *Death*. She superbly maintains her presence, reminding us all to seek out the beauty in each moment of life!

Death gives time its value. You've got a limited amount of time and a lot to do! It really is just a matter of intentionality. So, it's time to:

> ## *"Get busy living, or get busy dying."*

Naturally, even that quote is from another movie!

Which one? I'll give you a hint: *Morgan Freeman was in it.* Of course, that doesn't really narrow it down – Morgan Freeman is in nearly *every* movie!

Ok then, here's another hint: *Tim Robbins co-starred.*

You guessed it: *The Shawshank Redemption.*[iv]

Let's get busy *living!*

**"It comes down to a simple choice, really.
Get busy living, or get busy dying."**
– Andy Dufresne to Red in
The Shawshank Redemption

NOTES

i. See James 4:14 – Scripture taken from the HOLY BIBLE, NEW INTERNATIONAL VERSION® (NIV). Copyright © 1973, 1978, 1984 International Bible Society. Used by permission of Zondervan. All rights reserved.

ii. *Collateral Beauty*, directed by David Frankel (2016; Los Angeles, CA: New Line Cinema, Village Roadshow Pictures, 2017), DVD.

iii. Perhaps this list of "Love" questions sounds familiar to you? The Christian Apostle Paul, wrote the treatise on Love upon which these questions are based in his famous letter to the Church in Corinth in the 1st Century AD. 1 Cor 13:4-7. Scripture taken from the HOLY BIBLE, NEW INTERNATIONAL VERSION® (NIV). Copyright © 1973, 1978, 1984 International Bible Society. Used by permission of Zondervan. All rights reserved.

iv. *The Shawshank Redemption,* directed by Frank Darabont (1994; Los Angeles, CA: Castle Rock Entertainment, 1994), DVD

Chapter 4

The *Whys* Behind Your *Whats*

"He who has a strong enough why can endure any how."
— Friedrich Nietzsche

Your Bucket List

Take a moment to look out into your future. Reflect on the important future events, accomplishments, or milestones you're most looking forward to in life. Perhaps write them in your personal journal, or in the *Extraordinary Why Companion Workbook*, for later reflection.

Now, consider this question:

"Which future event, accomplishment, or milestone means the most to me?"

Let me give you a hint:

It's the one that makes you *emotional*. You get choked up, or really fired-up – excited. Or perhaps there's just one you can't get out of your mind; you keep ruminating on one in particular. Strong emotions like those are often signs your body gives to indicate what holds deepest meaning for you. Something 'moves' you *emotionally*, and so, if you allow it, that something will *move* you to *physically* take action.

Reflecting more deeply to explore such events, accomplishments, or milestones will transform you. If no such occurrence moves you immediately, ask yourself this question:

"If my funeral were sooner rather than later, and I could achieve or experience only one of these things, which would it be?"

Tough question? Sometimes. But, often, if we dwell on the question for just a short while, the answer comes.

Usually, if we go back and reapply the emotional litmus test to just the top events, there's often a standout among them – one thing that, if accomplished, makes the others more likely to occur. Or, perhaps achieving or experiencing one makes the others seem less important, or even irrelevant.

If there's a definite standout on your Bucket List for you, this is one of your *'Yonder Stars'* – "up and above the path you're traveling."

The *Whys* behind your *Whats*

Now, ask yourself *'Why?'* that event means so much to you.

Over the past decade, I've completed this exercise with thousands of people in hundreds of workshops. Typically, I conduct these workshops in group meetings or spousal retreats, often with CEO Peer Advisory Boards, Corporate Leadership Teams, or Boards of Directors. Sometimes, I do a slightly modified version with larger audiences in keynote presentations at conferences.

In these settings, *whats* that matter to people usually come quickly. In 3-5 minutes, most people come up with a compelling list of things they are most looking forward to in life, especially after we prime the pump by having them envision their own funeral beforehand. That 'death-perspective' connects us with *what* truly matters most.

The *whys*, however, often require coaxing to flesh them out fully.

Sometimes, a *first-pass* (top-of-head) **why** comes quickly. It doesn't require much introspection, particularly when participants cull the list of *whats* using the filter of emotional intensity. The real value of the *why*, though, often isn't discovered until we dig a little deeper.

Here is a brief list of the most common *whats* and first pass *whys* I hear in response to this two-part exercise of: 1) *What* future occurrence in your life means the most to you? 2) *Why* is that important to you?

Top 20 List of *Whats* and First Pass *Whys*

What's Most Important to Me?	Why Does it Matter to Me?
Raising my kids to be successful, contributing members of society.	This will mean I've done my job as a parent well.
Walking my daughter down the aisle at her wedding / Seeing my kids get happily married and have families of their own.	There's just something about that day that moves me – makes me think of all the days in my past with them, and all the days they has ahead.
Enjoying the 'empty nest' with my spouse or significant other.	We've been so busy raising kids and getting to this point that we need to focus on 'us' again.
Traveling the world with my partner, family, kids, or grandkids.	Some of our strongest memories have been formed around our times away as a family.
Being an active and involved grandparent for that next generation.	I was so busy when my kids were young that I missed a lot of stuff with them so I'm looking forward to doing it better with the next generation.
Celebrating a particular milestone (e.g. 25th or 50th) wedding anniversary.	There's a sense of accomplishment and family togetherness for us when we envision that day.
Living up to my full potential in the workplace.	I don't want to regret playing it too safe or 'selling-out' in any way.
Making a difference in my community somehow.	I know that life is not all about me and I want to give back.

What's Most Important to Me?	Why Does it Matter to Me?
Reconnecting with old friends or mentors.	I've lost touch over the years with people that made a big difference in my life. I'd like to thank them and rekindle those relationships.
Finishing well with my parents as they age and need my help in their final days.	They helped me become who I am today – I'd like to honor them. I know my kids are watching how I do this!
Finding answers to the bigger, deeper, more spiritual questions I have that still linger and/or growing in my faith more deeply.	I sense there's more to come after this life. I'm not sure I'm truly ready; or, I *sense* faith is what life is all about and I want to make sure I don't miss it while I'm here.
Completing a specific project, in the community or some civic association where I'm involved.	I know that if I don't, I will have failed to fulfill my purpose here.
Reconciling a broken relationship from my past and/or forgiving myself for past failings.	Lack of forgiveness has cost me in the past and I'd like to heal and move on, and/or I'm my own worst critic and I'd like to find peace with my imperfections.
Completing that degree that I never finished or seeing my kids graduate.	Feels like I quit my education too soon or I really want to see my kids pass this milestone for themselves so I'd like to be a good model.
Successfully handing off my business to the next generation.	That will mean that it survived me and I stewarded it well.
Retirement: Work becomes optional.	I'll have the time to do what I really want to do.
Building a retirement home in the place of my dreams.	It will serve as a place for me to enjoy with my spouse and extended family.
Achieving a particular job title.	I connect meaning to that milestone.
Achieving a specific net worth.	That number seems significant to me.
Completing a specific professional project.	That project is particularly meaningful to me.

That's a fairly solid list of things that truly matter in life!

Is there any overlap between this Top 20 List and yours? If so, highlight items on the list above that parallel those on your list.

Do you need to add anything to your list now that you've seen a few more ideas? Maybe you want to create your own list in your journal? If so, do it now. It's your life – don't miss the big stuff!

<u>Digging deeper into your *whys*</u>

The real value of the *why* often isn't discovered until we dig deeper. Think back to the *why* behind your 'Yonder Star.' Consider that *why* once again to get it freshly into your thinking. Now, take a step back from that *why* and ask *why* again:

"Why is THAT first-Pass *Why* important to me?"

This is your **second pass** why.

Take a moment to record one, or more, second-pass *whys* in your journal or in the *Extraordinary Why Companion Workbook.*

Sometimes, it comes relatively quickly. If so, great! You're on the verge of a breakthrough – one that will give you insight and inspiration for the journey ahead.

If not, perhaps one or more of the following prompters, summarized from the most popular answers I hear from people around the world, might prove helpful.

Is your *Yonder Star:*

An *education-related* milestone? Either for yourself or perhaps for one of your loved ones? Like: 'completing my college degree 'OR 'watching my kids graduate from high school or college?' If so, ask yourself: '*why* does education matter so much to me?'

A *relationship-centric* milestone? A landmark wedding anniversary for yourself and your partner perhaps? OR 'experiencing true 'oneness' with my spouse / partner.' If so, ask yourself: '*why* is that relationship so dear to me?'

A *parenting-centric* milestone? Like: 'walking my daughter down the aisle at her wedding' OR 'teaching my son to hunt/fish/play golf' OR 'teaching him what it really means to be a man' OR 'modeling for her what it means to be a truly successful woman in this complicated world in which we live.' If so, ask yourself: '*why* does being a good parent hold so much significance for me?'

A *grandchild-related* milestone? Like: 'I'm looking forward to teaching my grandchild how to quilt, knit, run, shoot, or surf?' If so, ask yourself: '*why* does the thought of being involved with my grandkids evoke so much emotion for me?'

A *travel-related* or *adventure-related* milestone? Like: 'seeing the world with my partner' OR 'experiencing some specific travel-related adventure with my wife, child or other key person in my life.' If so, '*why* does traveling seem so important to me?'

A *professional project* OR *career-related* milestone? Perhaps there's a project you know you *must* complete before you die or you will have failed to fulfill your purpose in life? Or, perhaps there's a career-defining job position or title you're particularly driven to achieve? If so, '*why* does professional success hold such a place of importance in my life?'

A *contribution-related* milestone? Like: 'I want to make a noticeable difference – live for a cause much greater than myself.' OR, 'I see so many hurting people in the world in some particular area and I know I must be part of the solution to that while I'm still here.' If so, ask yourself: '*why* does serving others get me so emotional?'

A *spiritually-related* milestone? Like: 'Discovering why I'm here on planet Earth – my purpose here', OR perhaps, 'I'm looking forward to seeing each of my children discover Truth for themselves.' If so, '*why* does discovering the answers to these deep spiritual questions seem all-important to me?'

Did the *'passing of your parents'* show up on your list? If so ask yourself: *'why* will that milestone be so emotional for me?'

Perhaps *reconnecting with old friends and/or mentors* appeared on your list of Top *Whats*? If so, *'why* do those friendships matter so much to me?'

Did a *money* or *financially-related goal* make your 'most important' list? If so *'why* does money hold such a prominent position in the list of things that drive me in life?'

Finally, perhaps it was a *retirement-related goal* that seemed most meaningful to you? If so ask yourself: *'why* does retiring from work to the next phase of my life motivate me so powerfully?'

Where do my *whys* come from?

What common themes do you notice in these 'why-prompting' questions?

If you answered that 'many of them seem to take me back to my past,' you're spot on! Why is that? Over the years I've discovered that often, our biggest, deepest, most compelling *'whys'* are often formed in our past.

Our strongest drivers, the most powerful ones in our life, often come from the families, the homes, in which we were raised.

Here's a profound truth:

The crucible that forged you often forges in you your biggest, deepest, most compelling 'whys'

Usually, for one of two reasons:

Something Modeled:

Sometimes, something very positive was present in your family of origin. An admirable character trait, a positive quality, was modeled well. You were loved and accepted unconditionally or a hard work ethic was exemplified your home. If so, that's a huge blessing!

This also comes with a great deal of responsibility: *"You're not about to be the one that messes it up for future generations."* A good model can create a level of expectation we feel we must live up to. It creates pressure.

That powerful example of the good, modeled for you in your early formative years, can create a very strong driver in you – it exists at the core of your being. It pushes you, drives you – consciously or unconsciously. Either way, it's there: urging you to live up to its wonderful, yet demanding, example.

Something Missing:

Sometimes, though, something you desired or needed in your home of origin was missing. Its *absence* can create an even more powerful driver than the *presence* of something.

Maybe you longed for unconditional love and acceptance but were regularly met with a demanding, performance-based love. A high expectation for perfection or perhaps the opposite: an apathetic or uncaring attitude towards you was regularly demonstrated.

Worse yet, yours may have been an abusive home environment that scarred you deeply.

In any of these circumstances, you can become fiercely committed to passing on a different legacy to your children than the one you received.

The profound absence of the good you longed for can also create a very strong driver at your deepest core. It too can push you, drive you – consciously or unconsciously.

In our home of origin, sometimes something was powerfully *modeled* for us. Sometimes, something was conspicuously *missing* for us. More often, a complex combination of both conditions existed.

So, if you're struggling at all to find the biggest, driving *whys* in your life today, let me encourage you to travel back down *'Memory Lane.'* In your mind, travel back in time to your own family of origin. You will find clues there for sure.

What's *really* driving you?

With the benefit of those additional insights from your past fresh in mind, ask *'why?'* one final time.

Can you think of something even bigger, more deeply connected to who you are at the core of your being? It was probably formed in your home of origin.

"Why are those Second-Pass Whys so important to me?"

What's one of the biggest, deepest, driving *whys* in your life as you currently see it now? This doesn't have to be perfect.

Of course, it may change over time for you. So, don't worry about 'getting it right.' Reflect and then write down just one:

My Deepest Driving *Why*

_____

_____

_____

_____

_____

_____

_____

There it is – good for you! Perhaps you were already aware of this driver, or perhaps it came to you as a revelation. Either way, taking the time to journey back to that point in your past where that driver was created is almost always a useful and enlightening exercise.

Taking time to write down your *whys* and articulating them clearly also has value. You're now more aware of the strongest motivators in your life. You're more attuned to the things that matter most to you .

There's great power in possessing such awareness!

In the next chapter, we'll travel back down *Memory Lane* one more time – for the purpose of learning from our past, of course!

First, I'll tell you about the man who first brought this concept of the *"Why Behind the What"* to life for most of the Western World.

Viktor Frankl – The power of *why*

Perhaps you've heard of a man named Viktor Frankl?

Frankl was an Austrian psychiatrist who, at the beginning of World War II, was interned by the Nazis at three different concentration camps, including Dachau and Auschwitz. From the moment he entered these horrific camps, he ruminated on this phrase:

> *"He who has a strong enough why can endure any how."*

Those words of Friedrich Nietzsche *literally* kept Viktor Frankl alive.

They gave him a sense of meaning, purpose. They helped him endure the most brutal regime of the 20th Century.

He wrote about his experiences in his landmark book *Man's Search for Meaning*. They could be summarized as follows:

'They took all my worldly possessions. They locked me away. They killed my parents. They forced my pregnant wife to abort our unborn child. Ultimately, they killed my wife too.'

Having lost everything in the crucible of this experience, Frankl discovered the one thing nobody could ever take away from him – *his freedom to choose his response* to what was happening to him.

That belonged to him and him alone!

That realization was revelatory because he had studied the works of one of his predecessors, a Russian psychiatrist named Ivan Pavlov. You remember Pavlov from your high school psychology class?

Yes! Pavlov and his famous … dogs!

The bell rings, the dogs look for food. The bell rings, the dogs look for food. Do this enough and there doesn't even have to be food present. The dogs will hear a ringing bell, will immediately begin to salivate, and will start looking for food.

Stimulus: the ringing bell. Reaction: look for food. Hardwired. Conditioned.

Prior to World War II, the psychological community believed that humans were exactly like Pavlov's dogs and could be conditioned. But Frankl learned this in the death camps:

'Dr. Pavlov, that's not true.'

The last of human freedoms is the ability to create a gap between stimulus and reaction, and into that gap put *personal choice*. Personal choice can convert a conditioned reaction into a **considered response.**

'The world MUST know what I've learned in this dismally dark place, so I'm getting out.'

Everybody in the camps had the goal of getting out of the camps: 'I'm getting out of here some day – that's *what* I'm going to do!'

Frankl put a really big *why* behind that goal: *Teaching the world* became his *extraordinary why* and his reason for surviving – His purpose. Everything he did from that moment forward guided him toward achieving that goal.

Each morning at roll call, instead of looking at the other emaciated prisoners all around him, instead of listening to the angry voices of the guards snarling and shouting at him, Frankl would walk out and simply stand there. He would envision himself standing in front of auditoriums filled with students, teaching them about the power they possessed to choose their response to the stimuli in their lives. Frankl was in that auditorium every morning.

Not everyone who had an *extraordinary why* made it out of the death camps. These camps were designed to make sure that you didn't. That was their purpose. But *the only* people who got out had a strong and compelling reason for doing so – one that made them emotional.

On your way to achieving those goals that matter so much to you in life, consider both your *what* and your *why*. If it's just a *what* without a *why* behind it that's so powerful you can literally feel it when you reflect upon it, here's what will happen:

You'll be sitting across the dinner table from that spouse, those kids, those grandkids who mean so much, and your smartphone will ring or vibrate. Instead of remaining fully present in that moment with those you hold most dear, you'll divert your attention to your device. Your life will be ruled by *urgency* – and you'll miss the potential opportunity to be significant.

I'm NOT saying that time with family should *always* come before time at work. There may be some professional project you're committed to achieving before you leave Earth or you know you will have failed to fulfill your purpose.

Then, it's those darling little grandchildren that can become the distraction. You'll have so much fun playing and spending time with them that you'll neglect your project and miss contributing something to the world that you were destined to achieve while you were here. It works both ways!

So, regularly consider the *whats* you know are connected to your biggest, deepest, most compelling *whys*. Frequently take time to connect emotionally to those goals. Feel them. Allow them to fill your being with passion and energy.

Then, you will have the fortitude to say 'No' to the urgent distractions of life because you'll be saying 'Yes' to what is truly most significant to you and the world around you.

Thank you, Dr. Frankl, for your life's work that significantly contributed to the world!

Now, close your eyes one more time and take a big, deep cleansing breath. We just talked about Nazis … remind your brain that everything is OK, right here, right now.

After that deep breath, reflect on this chapter – on your most meaningful relationships and on the most compelling *whys* in your life!

What's your why? Your Big Why?

"We long for love.
We wish we had more time.
We fear death."
— Howard (Will Smith)
in *Collateral Beauty*[ii]

NOTES

i. Viktor Frankl, *Man's Search for Meaning* (Boston, MA: 2006). First published in German in 1946 under the title *Ein Psycholog erlebt das Konzentrationslager*. Original English edition published by Beacon Press. 2008 UK Edition published by Rider, an imprint of Ebury Publishing, a Random House Group company. Copyright © 1959, 1962, 1984, 1992, 2004 by Viktor E. Frankl. Used by permission of the Estate of Viktor Frankl.

ii. *Collateral Beauty*, directed by David Frankel (2016; Los Angeles, CA: New Line Cinemas, Village Roadshow Pictures, 2017), DVD

Chapter 5

What's Holding You Back?

> *"We make peace with our past*
> *so it doesn't mess up our future."*
> *– Operating Principle #1 of a Seattle-based Vistage Group*

Your final moments

What will you be thinking about in your final moments on Earth?

In less than six short minutes, Long Island Emergency Medical Services Worker/First Responder, Matthew O'Reilly summarizes dozens of 'final moment' conversations to which he's been privy.

In his excellent TED Talk[i], called *"Am I dying?" The honest answer,"* O'Reilly talks about the three things he routinely hears after he's told people that they're about to die. Regardless of the person, these three themes seem to come up almost every time:

First (and Matthew says it's <u>always</u> first), is a desire **to forgive** *someone, or a need* **to seek forgiveness** *from someone.*

The second theme is this: 'Is anybody going to **remember me?***'*

The final theme: 'Wow! I've lived. Now I'm dying. Did anything I do while I was here…matter? Is the world any better because I was in it, or did I waste this gift called life? **Did I matter?**

We started this book by talking about your legacy. We even considered some of things you'd like those closest to you to say about who you were in their lives while you were here.

That's all about *remembrance*.

The very word *significance* in the book's subtitle connotes *meaning*. *Mattering*. Being relevant and not wasting this gift called life.

But we don't gain access to *forgiveness* except when we look back into our past. Your past is where you'll find the need to forgive, or seek forgiveness from, another.

So, let's take a quick trip down 'Memory Lane.'

A brief trip down 'Memory Lane'

Before we travel, let's remind ourselves why it can be productive to look at our past: to *learn* from it! We use our past to inform our future *ABCDs*: 'This *wrong stuff* back there didn't work so well for me.' 'This *right stuff*, on the other hand, worked pretty well.' Less of the former, more of that latter in the days ahead – that's why we're doing this.

Here's the question to start you off:

So far in life, what's been my biggest regret or disappointment?

A little advice before you get going, because sometimes I get pushback on the words *regret* and *disappointment*. I hear something like:

"I have no regrets or disappointments! Everything that ever happened to me made me the person I am today!"

I get that. There can be power in that kind of positive thinking. But it's not the most helpful thinking for this little trip.

Right now, if those words hang you up in anyway, use other words that give you mental access to past feelings of being *unfulfilled*. *Dissatisfied*. Or perhaps, '*something that you would change about your past if only you were able.*"

Don't overdo it, just ask yourself that question now and capture the first memory that springs to your mind.

So far in life, what's been my biggest regret or disappointment?

Continue reading when one memory comes to your mind.

The desire to skip over this difficult topic is natural: 'Why focus on the negative?' 'Let's leave the past in the past.' 'Let's focus on the positive and just move directly to strategies that help me identify and create my unique, extraordinary legacy.'

Yet, over the past decade, I've discovered a secret – a limitation that keeps people from achieving all they hope for in life. In my workshops and individual coaching settings, here's the nearly universal, limiting theme I've discovered:

> *Sometimes, something in your past*
> *keeps you stuck where you are.*

Some issue in your past that you haven't resolved. Some offense you still hold on to as a debt that's 'owed' to you.

Or, some wrong you've perpetrated that you haven't owned, atoned for, or for which you have not made amends. You have unfinished business so you are not 'complete' with yourself in the present moment of your life. Such things can hinder you. Such *unresolved wounds* can prevent you from progressing toward the legacy you'd really like to leave behind.

In the next few sections you'll learn a powerful strategy for making peace with your past – so it doesn't mess up your future. In order to move forward, though, you must first consider your *default legacy*.

Your default legacy

Shown below is the diagram I introduced back in Chapter 2. This time, I've added your *Personal Timeline* at the bottom and a couple familiar icons to the illustration:

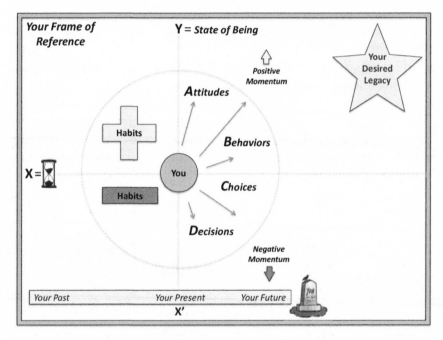

Figure 5.1

To recap and explain additional information shown in Figure 5.1:

You are in your present moment (X'). In any circumstance, a universe of possible future *ABCDs* surrounds you. Some will lead you closer to fulfilling your optimal legacy. Others will take you farther away. Over time, your habits will create positive momentum toward, or negative momentum away, from your desired legacy.

We ALL leave behind a legacy.

It may be an intentional legacy – one that you've considered deeply and have taken the time to shape. Alternatively, you may have never considered your legacy. That doesn't mean you're not going to have one.

You will, of course! It'll just be an unintentional legacy, what I like to call your *default legacy*. There are many definitions for the word default. But the most useful one, in our current context, comes from the world of computer programming:

default
[dih-fawlt]

- *Computers*: a value that a program or operating system assumes, or a course of action that a program or operating system will take, when the user or programmer specifies no overriding value or action.

Your *default legacy* is the one you will leave behind in the world if you take no overriding action to adjust it. It will be what it will be. It may or may not prove satisfying to you now or in your final moments.

Picture your *default legacy* as a cloud hovering somewhere in your current frame of reference. Where should it be placed horizontally?

While forged in your past, your *default legacy* isn't there anymore.

Remember, your legacy lives in *others* when you come to their heart and mind in the future. So, your *default legacy* currently exists only in the future. Therefore, horizontally, it will be to the right of where you presently are on your timeline.

Where should it be placed vertically? Its precise positioning varies by the individual *other* you've impacted on your journey. Its position is a product of your past *ABCDs* with respect to that other person.

Living an *extraordinary life of significance* requires a view of your default legacy that resides somewhere below *Your Desired Legacy*. Place your *default legacy* down and to the right of where you are in this moment.

This is shown in Figure 5.2, below.

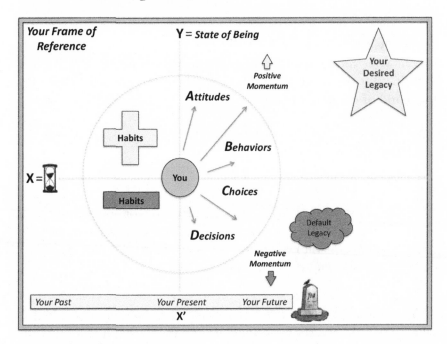

Figure 5.2

Because *Your Desired Legacy* is an aspirational *Yonder Star*, above your current path, there is distance between your default legacy and your desired one. That's the gap we're intentionally working to close on our epic journey.

Unresolved wounds in your past

You've now considered your default legacy's current positioning. Let's revisit this secret limitation that keeps many from achieving all they hope in life:

Often, something in your past keeps you stuck where you are.

I call such things – *unresolved wounds.* Issues, offenses, or debts we're hanging onto. Messes we've made that we haven't cleaned up. Some may be recent, others long-past. They may be top-of-mind, ever present. Some may operate in the background, buried deeply – or even suppressed completely from our consciousness.

Maybe they're something minor – inconsequential. Perhaps they're something big. Either way, we just can't shake their hold on us.

Picture them in Figure 5.3:

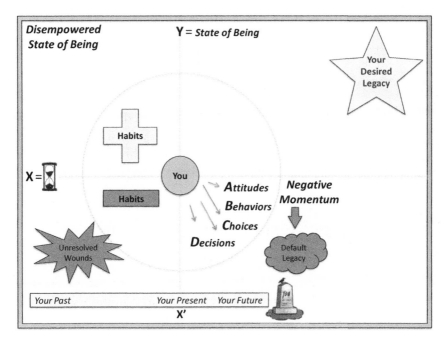

Figure 5.3

Unresolved wounds in our past can affect us in our present, negatively impacting our current *ABCDs.*

This puts us into a *Disempowered State of Being* that increases the *Negative Momentum* away from *Your Desired Legacy.* Such unresolved wounds can influence us so profoundly that they can shift your *default legacy* even lower. Living is such a Disempowered State of Being can even shorten your lifespan!

So, rather than moving full steam ahead toward defining and living into *Your Desired Legacy*, this is a good place to pause. Intentionally take time to identify and address any issues that may be holding you back.

> *Make peace with your past,*
> *so it doesn't hinder your future.*

When we do this, an amazing thing happens! We create *a clearing* around us in our present. We create a space in which we can breathe freely – space in which we can be *complete* with all things behind and with 'who we are' in the moment. From such a clearing, we're able to move forward much more powerfully than ever before.

To illustrate, I'll share the story of how I worked through one of my regrets with help from a trusted friend. It was an issue in my past, which became a hindrance in my present, and threatened to ruin my future. By working through it, I found forgiveness and freedom.

My story of past regret and disappointment

Every member of the family in which I was raised eventually spent some time being counseled by Larry – a professional family therapist. As I've already alluded, one doesn't grow up in a home with an actor and actress for parents without there being quite a bit of drama in the household, and not all of it the good kind!

I was the last member of my household to go see Larry. When I arrived in his office the first time, I was in my early 20s. He smiled broadly as he greeted me:

> *"Ahh, Brett! I've been waiting for you! I've worked with all the other members of your family, and now I get to take a crack at you!"*

These weren't his exact words, but that's the humorous way I choose to remember it. It was the beginning of a great relationship!

Over the past 30 years, I've seen a few other gifted counselors and have benefited enormously from that investment in myself.

About a decade ago, I walked into my current therapist's office – his name is Gene. As I walked through his door that afternoon, Gene got right down to business:

"Alright Pyle. Who do you need to forgive today?"

Always a great place to start a counseling session! At least with me, apparently, as I have a tendency to 'hold on' to things.

In response, I closed my eyes and asked my *conscience* that question:

Who do I need to forgive today?

Afterwards, I sat there and remained silent. Note this:

> *Your <u>conscience</u> will speak to you.*
> *You just need to give it time and space to do so.*

Surprisingly, that day, a few short minutes later, my dad came to mind.

"Got it – your dad. Why him? What particular memory did your conscience bring to your mind?" Gene asked.

I considered Gene's question, cast my mind back, and shared with Gene this particular memory from my past:

After Dad left the Broadway stage, he became a businessman and eventually launched a production company of his own. Later in life, Dad became a Turnaround CEO: a leader charged with turning around an unprofitable organization. Back at home in those days, from age 10 on, it was my job to take care of the yard.

Before Dad departed for his trips, he'd give me my instructions: 'Mow the yard, Brett. Weed the beds and the garden. Edge the sidewalks.'

I was the yard boy. Initially, I loved my job – I'd get paid to boot! Eventually, I started taking care of neighbors' yards too. I had my own business. It was pretty cool for a young kid.

Inevitably, though, Dad would return from his travels and we'd take 'a tour' around our yard. It was always a very special 'bonding time' for father and son! The yard could have been 99% perfectly manicured, but it never mattered. In my recollection, every single tour had this wonderful moment in which Dad would say:

"Hey! Isn't that a weed there? Right there. That's a weed. I thought we agreed you'd weed the yard? Now there's a weed! Take some pride in your work, son. Come on … where was your head?'

What began as constructive criticism soon became something very different. I started to hate the job I once loved.

Returning from my recollection of the past, to the present moment there in Gene's office that day, I finally answer his question directly:

"Gene, it's a little thing, but I never really enjoyed the 'Isn't that a weed?' moment on those tours. That's the memory that came to mind just now when you asked whom I needed to forgive today."

"Got it," said Gene. Then he asked: *"Did you forgive him?"*

I convinced him that I did, but something about my demeanor confused him.

"Ok. That does sound like forgiveness, Brett. But if you did that, you should be looking light and free. Like a burden has been lifted. Right now, you look like 'death-warmed-over.' Like a burden has been dropped on you. What's the problem?"

After what seemed like an eternity, I looked Gene in the eye and confessed:

"Here's the problem, Gene: I think I'm twice as bad with my own son as my dad ever was with me."

Wisely, Gene gave me a few moments to contemplate my words. I was overcome with emotion, thinking about my relationship with my then, 11-year-old, son Jonathan. Once I composed myself, Gene said:

"I suspect that on one of those walks around your yard, I bet you said to your dad ... hey, maybe not even out loud. Maybe you just said it to yourself. But I bet it sounded something like:"

"I hate you, Dad."

It didn't take two seconds for my memories to go back to those moments in my past. In Gene's office that day, I heard myself speak the words again. I felt them well up in my tight throat before I choked them out in an anger I had never before given myself permission to express:

"I hate you, Dad! Nothing I ever do is good enough for you. Nothing! I will never be like you!"

Gene let those words hang in the air for what seemed like an additional eternity.

"Ok Brett," he said very matter-of-factly. *"That's the problem."*

"What do you mean?" I replied.

What Gene said and did next changed my life:

"Brett. We're called to honor our mother and father. We're called to honor them whether they were worthy of honor or not. Their behavior isn't part of that equation. Our role, as the child, is to honor our parents. When we dishonor them, by saying something like 'I hate you,' and then we make a strong vow that sounds anything like 'I will never be like you,' we're actually breaking a law."

> *"Dishonor your parents,*
> *vow strongly that you'll never be like them,*
> *and in the <u>spiritual</u> realm*
> *you curse yourself to become exactly like them!"*

"This is why perfectionists beget perfectionists, Brett. It's why addicts beget addicts, why abusers abuse people, and hurt people hurt people."

Earlier, we spent some time reflecting upon the legacy we'll leave behind to our descendants and the world that survives us. While we're here on the 'X' of life, the time between the two dates that'll be on our gravestone, we're recipients of legacies too, though, aren't we?

We receive our parents' legacies, our grandparents' legacies, and our great grandparents' legacies. All the way back – three, even four, generations.

We even have a word for the sum of all those legacies we receive – a *heritage*. **We receive a heritage – we pass on a legacy.** While we're alive, we are given this opportunity:

> *Take the good elements of our heritage,*
> *the eulogy-worthy elements of our heritage,*
> *share them with to the world,*
> *and pass them onto the next generation.*

"Gene. What do I do about this?"

"Two things. First, there's somebody else besides your dad that you need to forgive. Who do you think that might be?"

"I'm thinking you're going to say myself, Gene. Am I right?"

"You're spot on, my friend!"

Then, Gene gave me a gift. He looked me in the eyes and said:

"Brett. You've dishonored your dad. I've heard your confession. You shouldn't have done it. That was wrong."

After letting that soak in for a few moments, he added:

Welcome to the human race!" I forgive you. Do you want that forgiveness Brett?"

A long pause ensued as many thoughts coursed through my head. I really had forgiven my dad, so there wasn't any more bitterness there. Yet, I still had hesitancy about accepting forgiveness so readily. I felt unworthy of forgiveness.

Eventually, I relented:

"Yes, Gene. I absolutely want, and accept, that forgiveness! I think I've been carrying that around for a while."

"I know you have, Brett." Gene confirmed.

Click!

In THAT second, for the first time in what had then been 45 years of my life, a small, but definite gap formed in my heart.

In between *the stimulus* of having been parented by a demanding perfectionist and *my reaction* of parenting as a demanding perfectionist, a gap was created in my heart.

Up until that moment, I was Pavlov's Dog.

Conditioned. Trained very well for eighteen plus years in the crucible in which I was formed – the home in which I was raised. But through the act of forgiveness, and the act of receiving and accepting forgiveness, the gap emerged.

I was now free to choose a different response IF I wanted to do so. Immediately, I felt the burden lift. This incredible *lightness of being free* was breathed into my spirit.

I was *inspired*.

inspire
[in-spire]

1. a: to influence, move, or guide by supernatural inspiration
   b: to exert an animating, enlivening, or exalting influence on

2. a: (archaic) : **to breathe into** or upon
   b: (archaic): to infuse (something, *such as life*) by breathing

I gave, and accepted, forgiveness for a past wrong. As a result, I was inspired … *Life* was breathed into me in that moment! Now, I was almost elated as I glimpsed a new way forward.

"What's the other thing, Gene? Whatever it is, I promise I will do it!"

"I know you will," Gene replied. *"Go make it right with your boy."*

Somehow, I knew he would say that.

I drove home and began the process of making it right with my son. That process included a heart-felt, emotional conversation with my boy in which I uttered these words:

"Son, it's not okay for me to parent you in a way that makes you feel you have to be perfect to earn my love. That's wrong. I'm wrong! Will you please forgive me?"

I was crying. He was crying. It was a sloppy scene. In the midst of that mess, I hugged him close and felt his head start to bob up and down in an affirmative motion.

"Yeah, Dad. I forgive you," he choked out.

The tenseness left his body as I hugged him even tighter. I'm thankful that even my awkward approach to the whole conversation seemed to give him a much-needed release.

"Thanks, Bud. I appreciate that. I really do! I __am__ sorry, and I promise you I will do better from now on."

We broke our embrace and dried our eyes. I made a light-hearted wisecrack about it being ok for 'Real Men' to cry before we got on with our evening.

The next morning, *lightness* showed up in our relationship. He crawled up into my lap and we started wrestling, the way a father and son are supposed to do. We hadn't done that in months. It was in this lightness that I realized something profound: *I didn't need my boy's forgiveness. I was fine. HE needed to forgive me.*

As his dad, I just needed to make it easy for him to do so by apologizing and asking for his forgiveness.

> *I was parenting for Perfection ...*
> *Perfection is the enemy of Good, let alone Excellent.*

Until that moment, the message playing inside by son's head probably sounded like this: *"I hate this guy ... I will never be like him!"*

If I didn't own my behavior and intentionally create an opportunity for him to forgive me, he would invariably pass on the same curse to *his* son someday. The curse would keep on going down through the generations!

Today, about a decade later, I'm slowly getting better as a parent. I'm not perfect. I've given up trying to be – that was half the problem!

Offering and embracing forgiveness

I tell you this emotional, way too sappy story for one reason:

If Matthew O'Reilly is right, and the first thing you're going to be thinking about in the final moments of your life is *'Who do I need to forgive?'* or *'From whom do I need to seek forgiveness?'* Why wait?

Honestly. Why wait? Why carry around a heavy burden any longer than you must? Take a moment. In the quietness you've created for yourself, take a moment and ask yourself this question:

"Whom do I need to forgive?"

Asked another way:

"Right now, in this moment, am I at peace with absolutely everyone, or am I harboring any degree for bitterness or resentment towards anyone, living or dead, in my past?"

Take time, here and now, to reflect on that all-important question.

If someone's coming to your mind right now, especially if you're pushing someone out of your mind, with this thought:

"Not that person. They wronged me!"

Then, yeah: That's the person! The forgiveness is not for *them*. It's for *you*!

Bitterness and resentment toward another have no effect on them, and they're killing you. Literally. Shortening your life. There's medical evidence.[ii]

Understandably, you may not *want* to forgive certain people. That's a different matter entirely. But, right now, we're not talking about having the *desire* to forgive. We're also not talking about whether that person(s) *deserves* forgiveness.

For now, ask *who in your past do you need to forgive* to free you from any bitterness or resentment that might be consuming you?

Perhaps no one is coming to mind? You might be honestly asking yourself that question and absolutely no names, or faces, are coming to your mind. That can be a great way to live, free from past hindrances!

If that's the case for you, consider this: *I may not be harboring any bitterness or resentment toward any other person, but...*

"Is there anyone who once was in my life but is now 'dead' to me? Anyone I've just written-off because of a situation that occurred between us?"

In the space below, jot down the names (or initials if you prefer) of whomever your conscience brought to mind:

_____

_____

_____

Wonderful – good work!

Now ask yourself this final question:

"Have I wronged anyone or hurt someone and need to seek their forgiveness?"

Take time as you consider that question, and then jot down the names or initials of whomever your conscience has now brought to mind:

_____

_____

_____

If you've recorded any names or initials in the spaces above, good for you – that's hard work. You don't have to 'fix' these things right now. Now, we're simply noticing them.

Charles F. Kettering, the famed American inventor, holder of over 300 patents, founder of Delco and head of research for General Motors for 27 years, once famously said:

> *"The problem well-stated is a problem half solved."*

That's the good news associated with the work you've just completed: You're halfway to the solution that will set you free!

Congratulations!

The even better news is this:

The other half of the solution is 100% within your own power!

Most people are unaware of this transformative truth. We'll cover that truth, *the key that unlocks the door to freedom,* in the next chapter.

Prisoner of War #1:   *"Have you forgiven your captors yet?"*

POW #2:   *"No! Never!"*

POW #1:   *"Then it seems they still have you in prison, don't they?"*

— *Spirituality and Health* magazine, Winter 1999

NOTES

i. Matthew O'Reilly, *"Am I dying? The Honest Answer,"* filmed September, 2014 in Long Island, New York, TED Video, 5:33, https://www.ted.com/speakers/matthew_o_reilly

ii. Dr. Dick Tibbits. *Forgive to Live – How Forgiveness Can Save Your Life – 10th Anniversary Expanded and Revised Edition.* (Altamonte Springs, Florida: Florida Hospital Publishing, 2006). Copyright © Dick Tibbits, 2006, 2016. Used by permission of AdventHealth Press.

In this landmark book, Dr. Dick Tibbits shares the medical evidence he's presented at the National Institutes of Health, Harvard University, The Mayo Clinic, Duke University, Loma Linda University, and Stanford University.

Dr. Tibbits designed and conducted a study to "investigate whether forgiveness could have measurable health benefits." He took participants, all of whom had been diagnosed with stage 1 hypertension, through "an eight-week program that taught them the art and practice of forgiving."

A psychological test that measured anger and hostility was also given to all participants.

At the end of the eight-week study, Dr. Tibbits had collected a lot of data. It demonstrated that individuals with high blood pressure and elevated anger who practiced forgiveness "succeeded both in reducing their anger and lowering their blood pressure. Beyond that, participants spoke a lot about improved relationships and reinvesting in life. Forgiveness really worked!"

Chapter 6

Creating Your Clearing

"Forgiveness is the process of
reframing your anger and hurt from the <u>past</u>,
with the goal of recovering your peace in the <u>present</u>,
and revitalizing your purpose and hopes for the <u>future</u>."
— Dr. Dick Tibbits

<u>What forgiveness is NOT and what it IS</u>

Forgiveness is the key that unlocks the door to personal freedom.

Earnestly seeking forgiveness from another, or willingly granting forgiveness to another, creates a 'clearing' in *your* life. It's one of the few forces so powerful that it can literally change the world.

With so much positive potential, one would think people would be actively searching for opportunities to practice forgiveness and unleash its benefits in their lives.

Yet, if you look at the world around you, clearly this isn't the case today. As a society, we seem to be getting increasingly more offended by others, not less so.

Why? Perhaps it's because we, as a society, have become so fixated on our own *rights* as individuals that we're less likely to see, and own, our own *wrongs*, much less forgive the wrongs of others?

Or, maybe it's simpler than that. Perhaps *forgiveness* is simply misunderstood?

Let's begin with there by describing what forgiveness ISN'T and what it IS. Look at the *Summary Table on Forgiveness* shown in Figure 6.1. Read each line item carefully in both columns. Highlight any items that strike you as unusual or counter-intuitive.

Summary Table on Forgiveness

Forgiveness is NOT ...	Forgiveness IS ...
Saying what happened in the past is OK.	A choice to change who you will be in the future.
Letting another person 'off the hook.'	Surrendering judgment to a greater authority.
Telling someone else you've forgiven them.	A private act between you and your conscience.
Agreeing to trust the person going forward.	Embracing health in the present and future.
Inviting an ongoing relationship.	An independent, powerful act you do alone.
Something you 'feel' like doing.	An act of will – independent of desire.
Something you do for another person.	A gift you give to yourself.
Forgetting what happened in the past.	Remembering you've CHOSEN to forgive.
Contingent on the other party's remorse.	Independent of the other's sorrow or remorse.
Reconciliation, which requires two parties.	100% in your control, independent of others.
A broad, sweeping, generic action.	A response to a specific offense in the past.
A 'once and done' thing.	A process that evolves over time.

Figure 6.1

Where are *you* on this topic of forgiveness?

Where are you right now with respect to the possibility that *forgiveness* might play a useful role for you in your life?

Do most statements seem obvious or familiar to you? If so, great! The rest of this chapter may be a refresher, providing you with the opportunity to take a brief personal inventory of the current state of your relationships to assess if any forgiveness might be helpful.

Alternatively, if you highlighted a number of different statements in the table that struck you as odd, unusual, or just plain wrong, perhaps you might wish to dive even deeper into this topic? If so, let me encourage you to follow along in the *Extraordinary Why Companion Workbook.* There's a lot more detail about each item in that book. There are also several exercises you can work through to apply these concepts to your life to create your own clearing.

Offering forgiveness to another

Here's a straightforward process for offering forgiveness when you've been offended. Note that NONE of this work involves the offending party.

- **Recall** a specific offense from your past.
- **Feel the pain** and emotion associated with the offense.
- **Acknowledge you've chosen to judge** for that offense.
- **From the place of pain**, take the next five steps:

1) **Choose now to forgive** the other: release them from your own judgment going forward; surrender them to the supreme judge who can, and will, judge them vastly more objectively than you.

2) **Confess**, to yourself and to a trusted friend, **that you have judged another**. Acknowledge that it's in your nature to do so and that you'd like to be better than you are in your natural state.

3) **Forgive yourself** for having done so: 'Welcome to the human race!' You're *not* perfect.

4) **Be willing to change** your attitudes, behaviors, choices, and decisions from this point forward. Find an accountability partner to help you do so.

5) **Forgive and** *remember*: If/when the memory of the offense subsequently occurs, resist the temptation to return to the role of judge. Rather, accept the recurrent memory as a 'gift.' It's an opportunity to remind yourself that you have chosen to forgive the other for the offense. Remember and make the same choice to forgive once again.

You may have to repeat this process for the same offense. Maybe even frequently at first. Over time, however, the need to do so will diminish. Eventually, you will get completely free from the memory and the bitterness and resentment will abate.

Seeking forgiveness from another

Here is a process for seeking forgiveness from others when you know, think, or just suspect you may have offended or hurt another.

1) **Prepare** for a conversation with the other person by considering how your attitude, behavior, choice, or decision may have hurt the other person. Consider how you would react if the tables were turned. Allow yourself to *feel* whatever emotions you might have experienced if you had been offended in a similar way.

2) **Get physically present** with the other person. Face-to-face is best. On the phone is next best, so they can hear your voice and tone. A letter, email, or other written form is least preferred since it lacks tone, which usually carries more of the message than words alone. **OR,** if the other person has passed away or physical presence isn't possible:

Get *spiritually* **present** with them. Because forgiveness is an act that occurs in the spiritual realm, you don't have to be physically present with another person to seek forgiveness from them if they are deceased.

3) **Concisely express your concern** that you believe you may have hurt or offended them. Describe why you think so including how you might have felt if you had been on the receiving end of that attitude, behavior, choice, or decision.

4) **Ask how they're feeling** about the interaction in question and **Listen intently** to their response. The following suggestions should help you respond appropriately to their response to your overture:

IF they express **they *were not* hurt** or offended (or they don't even remember the event):
- **Express relief**: *"Oh good. I was concerned that I may have hurt you. That's the last thing I'd want to do. I'm glad that's not the case."*
- **Affirm** how much you value your relationship with them.
- **Offer them ongoing permission** to let you know if any of your future attitudes, behaviors, choices, or decisions ever offends or hurts them.

IF they express that **they *were* hurt** or offended:
- **Acknowledge** the hurt, pain or emotion and its legitimacy. *"Wow. That's what I thought. That must have hurt. I probably would have felt similar to that if someone had done that to me."*
- **Apologize**. *"I'm sorry, [Name]."*
- **Ask for forgiveness**. *"Will you please forgive me?"*

IF they **DO** acknowledge your apology, accept it, and offer you forgiveness:
- **Thank them**. *"Thank you. I really appreciate you for offering your forgiveness. That means a lot to me."*
- **Ask** how they might want you to handle similar situations if they recur in the future so that you don't repeat the hurt or offense.
- **Listen** intently to their response and respond appropriately.

IF they **DON'T** acknowledge your apology, accept it, or offer forgiveness:

- **Don't judge or criticize** their response. They are where they are at the moment and you probably can't change that just because you're sorry you hurt them. Instead, **listen intently** to their response (or lack of response).
- **Express understanding and ask for more information** about how what you did occurred to them, if they're willing to offer it. Again, **acknowledge** that you're aware that you've hurt or offended them.
- **Repeat** that you want them to know that you do regret doing so and are truly sorry for the offense.
- **Express hope** that, one day, they're able to forgive you.

If you take these steps from genuine, heartfelt sorrow for having hurt someone, you instantly "break free" from regret. Regardless of their acceptance, response, or lack thereof, *you* **are set free.**

Seldom is it an easy process – especially if the wound is significant, deep-seated, or complex. So, whether you're seeking to forgive another, or are seeking forgiveness from another, **get some assistance with the process.** To guide you through the process, seek support from:

- a professional counselor
- a therapist
- a trained spiritual advisor

Even if the thought of this experience is uncomfortable to you, don't let that discomfort deter you from trying it. If you've been carrying a burden for years, why miss an opportunity to set it down, let it go, and get free? Remember:

Transformation takes place outside of our comfort zone, not in it!

Many have experienced great freedom from going through a process like this one. But, of course, the choice is yours!

Why forgiveness is so powerful

> *By forgiving, or seeking forgiveness, you set yourself free from a jail of your own creation.*

Remember this diagram from the last chapter?

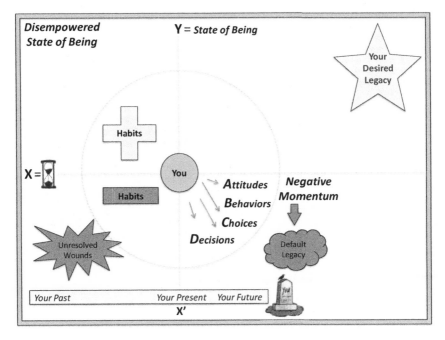

Figure 6.2

When you confront and address one of the *unresolved wounds* from your past, it effectively 'disappears' and loses its grip on you.

One at a time, repeat this work with each specific offense you're holding onto. Ultimately, you'll break completely free from the negative influences in your past. Those *unresolved wounds* from your past will cease holding you back – you will have resolved them. In so doing, you create *a clearing* around yourself in the present:

clearing
[kleer-ing]

1: the process of becoming *clear* (see below)
2: a tract of land, as in a forest, that contains no trees or bushes

clear
[kleer]

Various definitions:

- free from darkness, obscurity, or cloudiness; light of a *clear* day.
- free from confusion, uncertainty, or doubt: *clear thinking*.
- free from anything that would disturb or blame: *clear conscience*.
- free from suspicion of guilt or complicity: *cleared of the crime*. serene; calm; untroubled: he had *a clear brow*.
- free from obstructions or obstacles; open: *clear view; clear path*.

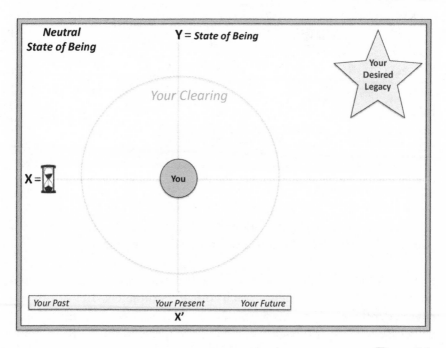

Figure 6.3

In such a clearing, you can exist in the present moment, free from hindrances of your past.

You can be fully present – at peace.

Mindful – in the moment.

From such a *clearing*, you are now free to choose the most useful *ABCD* – the one most appropriate for the present moment. You are no longer 'Pavlov's Dog,' conditioned to *react* to circumstances from past experiences. Rather, you have entered into an *Empowered State of Being*. You are now capable of *responding* to circumstances from a higher plane – a plane that has a clear view of *Your Desired Legacy*.

No longer haunted and hindered by the ghosts of your past, you can now choose better attitudes, behave in more positive ways, see a wider variety of choices available to you, and make better decisions. As you do, your relationships will invariably improve and you'll apply *Positive Momentum* on your *default legacy*. It will invariably shift upwards:

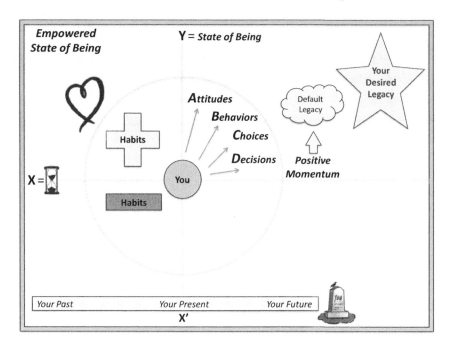

Figure 6.4

Having resolved wounds from your past, your present actions will be free from their negative influence. Your trips down 'Memory Lane' will take on a different quality. You may see moments of *Love* that you previously overlooked – times when love was offered to you or you freely gave it to others. Gratitude will fill in those places that before were occupied by bitterness.

Remember, this is not work you do for others so they'll say nice things about you. This is work you do for *you*. Conceivably, as you release the bitterness and resentment from your past, your lifespan may even extend out farther into the future!

Over time, you'll learn to remain in your clearing. To maintain it – strive to live in continual peace with everyone in the world around you. It's not about getting it perfect. It's about owning it when you don't get it perfect. Seeking forgiveness when you hurt others. Offering forgiveness freely to others when they offend you.

Which brings us to our final point about the *power of forgiveness*.

> *By embracing a lifestyle marked by forgiveness, you create the possibility that <u>others</u> might also get free from bitterness and resentment.*

Remember, it can be easier to forgive someone for an offense if you know, *they* know that what they did was hurtful to you, and you know *they* are sorry for the pain they caused. By having these conversations with them, they become aware of your remorse. They may not immediately respond favorably to your overture. Nonetheless, it will impact them.

By taking these steps, you free yourself <u>and</u> create the possibility that they too might one day get free. You remain the *primary beneficiary* of your decision to forgive another or seek forgiveness from another. AND, *others* become *additional beneficiaries* of your decision.

When a *physical* door is opened, people are free to pass through in both directions. So, it is with the *spiritual Door of Forgiveness* – when one person opens it, both people become free to pass through.

The other person may or may not decide to make that choice. If they don't, then only *you* break free. But they may decide to offer you forgiveness; they may decide to genuinely seek forgiveness from you for wrongs they feel they have done. IF they do, then the possibility of *reconciliation* is created.

> *Forgiveness requires only one person to act.*
> *Reconciliation takes two.*

You can't control the decisions others choose to make. But you CAN control whether or not you offer them the choice!

Forgiveness can change the *world*

A final story to illustrate the *world-changing* power of forgiveness:

I spent most of my career working in the Oil & Gas industry. I worked for Amoco Oil Company until BP eventually acquired us in 1999 in what was then the largest industrial merger in history. Shortly after the merger, my family and I left our home in suburban Chicago to take a role at the corporate headquarters in London.

One morning, there was an announcement that we were to have a very special guest come speak to us over the lunch hour. Noon rolled around and nearly a thousand of us packed into the corporate auditorium. Our CEO, John Browne, walked out on stage and said:

"Ladies and gentlemen, a man who needs no introduction."

A hush fell over the crowd as our CEO walked off the stage. An air of excitement and anticipation filled the room.

After a brief pause, Nelson Mandela walked out onto the stage. An audible gasp emerged from us all! We were in the presence of extraordinary greatness and we knew it.

Mandela gave a relatively short speech. Here's the essence:

"BP, I'm here to thank you.

During the years of apartheid, many Western countries and companies boycotted South Africa. This placed an enormous financial burden on us at a time we were already hurting. It made a bad situation even worse.

BP, you were one of the few Western countries that not only did NOT boycott us, but you increased your investment in our nation. That helped. Thank you.

Not only did you continue to invest in us, but you also appointed a black man to be BP's Country Manager for South Africa. At that time, my nation needed to see men and women of color in positions of leadership. That helped a great deal too. I'm here to thank you for believing in us – for supporting us. Thank you!"

Even more impactful than the speech was the man's *presence.* Here was a man that *literally* changed the world. Now, he was present in our midst. Mandela walked off the stage and positioned himself at the exit door to the auditorium. There he waited until all of us walked past him. He looked us each in the eye as he shook our hand and said, "Thank you," to the first … "Thank you," to the next … "Thank you," to yet another, until we had all passed by. He thanked us personally as if we each had something to do with BP's decision so many years ago!

The man changed the world by first spending *twenty-seven years* in prison on Robben Island, Pollsmoor Prison, and Victor Verster Prison. Not in a prison of his own making, but in prisons of man's making.

He was arrested in 1962 for conspiring to overthrow The State and was sentenced to life imprisonment. When he entered prison in 1964, Mandela had been labeled a *'terrorist'* for the actions he, and the African National Congress (ANC), had been taking. He spent the next twenty-seven years in jail working on the one and only thing he could control … *his own heart.*

Amid growing domestic unrest, international political pressure and fears of a racial civil war, President F. W. de Klerk released Mandela in 1990. By that time, Mandela was a kinder, gentler soul than anyone expected.

He was once quoted as saying:

> *"As I walked out the door toward the gate that would lead to my freedom, I knew if I didn't leave my bitterness and hatred behind, I'd still be in prison."*

Together, Mandela and de Klerk led efforts to end the 42-year long system of apartheid, which institutionalized racial segregation and discrimination in South Africa. In 1993, Mandela and de Klerk were jointly awarded the Nobel Peace Prize for their efforts.

The first-ever, multiracial general election in South Africa occurred in 1994. In that election, Mandela became the first President of "a united, democratic, non-racial, and non-sexist South Africa." In his Inaugural Address on May 10th, 1994, Mandela pledged to lead his country "out of the valley of darkness" to become "a rainbow nation, *at peace with itself* and the world."

Mandela's leadership was rooted in the belief that the problems facing his nation were far too big and *went back far too many generations* for them to be solved by conventional methods and negotiations.

Essentially, his life and leadership message to South Africa was this:

There's only one force powerful enough on Earth to heal us as a nation. It's called forgiveness. We must forgive!

Mandela didn't just preach forgiveness; he modeled it. He honored his former jailers (Christo Brand, Jack Swart, and James Gregory), with invitations – some to his inauguration, others to a dinner marking the 20th anniversary of his release from prison.[i]

In his book *Long Walk to Freedom*, Mandela wrote:

"Men like Swart, Gregory, and Warrant Officer Brand reinforced my belief in the essential humanity even of those who had kept me behind bars for the previous twenty-seven and a half years.[ii]*"*

In 1995, shortly after his election, Mandela invited his former prosecutor, Percy Yutar for a kosher lunch at the presidential mansion. After the lunch, Mr. Yutar, who once accused Mr. Mandela of being "a Communist stooge plotting a bloody revolution," pronounced the president "a saintly man.[iii]"

Mandela invested his presidency doing all he could to bring about the full reconciliation his country so badly needed. He even enlisted the Springboks, the South African national team, on a mission to win the 1995 Rugby World Cup. That story is inspiringly retold in the 2009 Warner Bros. film *Invictus*,[iv] starring Morgan Freeman as Mandela and Matt Damon as Springbok team captain, François Pienaar.

Few symbols captured the disdain white South Africans held for Mandela and the ANC more than the hated green Springbok jersey. At home matches, black South Africans were made to stand in pens to watch the games while white South Africans enjoyed the match seated comfortably in the stands. Nonetheless, the pens were always full of fans, cheering for whoever was playing *against* the Springboks.

Mandela was never one to miss an opportunity to model the need for, and power of, forgiveness and reconciliation. At the World Cup final match in 1995, he donned a green Springbok jersey. As he presented the World Cup trophy to South African captain Pienaar, wearing that jersey, he delivered a powerful message to his ANC colleagues: *'It is time to set aside enmity and become a united Rainbow Nation.'*

Nelson Mandela! He, literally, changed the world. He did so by demonstrating and modeling forgiveness that leads to reconciliation. Forgiveness. It can change the world! It has to begin with someone. Mandela asked: Why not me?

Why not you?

Resources to help

It often helps to work with an uninvolved, independent third party as you go through this process. Professional therapists are trained in this practice and can be an invaluable resource as you work through the tougher issues in your past.

Other resources I recommend to help you with the process of forgiveness include:

Forgive to Live[v] – Dr. Dick Tibbits
The Shack[vi] – William P. Young, the book and the movie!
Brain Savvy Leaders[vii] – Charles Stone
Walking Through Fire Without Getting Burned[viii] – Kirby King

If you've gotten this far, you've created a clearing for yourself. Or, at least, you now hold the key for doing so! Ready to step into *your extraordinary future?*

Take a few good, deep cleansing breaths. When you're ready, turn to the next chapter and we'll resume our journey from your clearing.

*"The time for the healing of the wounds has come.
The moment to bridge the chasm that divides us has come.
The time to build is upon us."*
– *Nelson Mandela*

NOTES

i. Nicol, Mike. 2011. *Nelson Mandela's Warders*. https://www.nelsonmandela.org/images/uploads/Nelson_Mandelas_Warders.pdf

ii. Nelson Mandela, *Long Walk to Freedom* (London: Abacus, 1995), 672.

iii. Goldman, Ari. L "Percy Yutar, 90, Prosecutor of Mandela in South Africa." *The New York Times* (2002): https://www.nytimes.com/2002/07/21/world/percy-yutar-90-prosecutor-of-mandela-in-south-africa.html

iv. *Invictus*, directed by Clint Eastwood (2009; Los Angeles, CA: Warner Bros. and Spyglass Entertainment, 2010), DVD.

v. Dr. Dick Tibbits. *Forgive to Live – How Forgiveness Can Save Your Life – 10ᵗʰ Anniversary Expanded and Revised Edition*. (Altamonte Springs, Florida: Florida Hospital Publishing, 2006). Copyright © Dick Tibbits, 2006, 2016. Used by permission of AdventHealth Press.

vi. William P. Young, *The Shack* (Newbury Park, CA: Windblown Media, FaithWords, Hodder & Stoughton 2007). *The Shack*, directed by Stuart Hazeldine (2017; Santa Monica, CA: Summit Entertainment and Netter Productions, 2017), DVD.

vii. Charles Stone, *Brain Savvy Leaders* (Nashville, TN: Abingdon Press, 2015). Charles Stone, "What Unforgiveness Does to Your Brain," Charles Stone, Stonewell Ministries, August 15, 2019, https://charlesstone.com/what-unforgiveness-does-to-your-brain/

viii. Kirby King, *Walking Through Fire Without Getting Burned*. (ISBN-13: 978-0578511092. 2019). Copyright © Kirby King, 2019.

Chapter 7

Identity – Who Are You, Really?

"Most men lead lives of quiet desperation ..."
– Henry David Thoreau

" ... They die with their voice still inside of them."
– Ralph Waldo Emerson

We find our identity in community

I often deliver my *Extraordinary Why* workshop to Vistage[i] member CEOs and business owners at their monthly board meetings. Sometimes spouses and significant others attend – especially when they take retreats.

In October 2017, I was asked to conduct one such spousal retreat for the Vistage Board chaired by my friend, Mike Akers.

Two weeks before the retreat, Mike received devastating news.

He had been diagnosed with an inoperable, late grade IV, glioblastoma multiforme tumor in his brain. Without treatment, he had 3 months to live – with treatment, maybe a year.

I called him up a couple of days later:

"Mike – tough news! I'm so sorry. How you doing?"

Optimistically, he answered:

"I'm hanging in there. Hey Brett, I'm glad you called! Let's talk about my group's retreat that's coming up. You ready to inspire them all with your workshop?"

It was 'classic Mike': thinking about others even during personal crisis.

Since the CEOs' spouses would be attending the retreat, Mike asked his wife, Trudy, to join us on the call. Somewhat hesitantly, I described the end-of-life perspective I often use in workshops to help people identify and connect to their purpose.

After I described the 'Funeral Exercise' I planned to use, Trudy said:

"Wow, Mike ... what do you think?"

Without hesitation, Mike responded:

"Oh you gotta come! I've already called all my group members, so everybody knows about my diagnosis. But it'll be our first time together since the news. This is perfect timing!"

"Trudy ... you okay with this?" I asked tentatively, to make sure Mike's enthusiasm and willingness to 'go there' with his group didn't make her too uncomfortable.

"Of course!" Trudy responded. Then added: *"It's the right thing to do."*

The morning of the workshop arrived. There was heaviness in the air as the couples arrived in the meeting room at the hotel. The gloom was palpable. No one knew what to say or how to act.

It was an awkward scene – until Trudy broke the ice:

"Folks, I know you're sad. Mike and I are pretty sad too. But give yourselves permission today, to laugh – to be joyful! Without these 'lows' in life we don't fully appreciate the 'highs.' And, if we take away the 'highs,' we don't learn all that these 'lows' have to teach us. So, give yourselves permission to experience the full range of emotions that come over you during our time together."

It was such a powerful thing to say. It was the gift the group most needed in that moment. She gave us all permission to become fully human again.

Mike brought some deep insights of his own that day too. Right after the funeral exercise he said:

"Well, if we had done that exercise three weeks ago, it would have seemed kind of 'theoretical' to me. But it's pretty darn real for me in this moment!"

Everyone laughed at the truth Mike nonchalantly offered with that statement. It was 'pretty darn real' for us all that day!

Mike received his cancer diagnosis on what was the 20th anniversary of when he and Trudy had buried their 21-year-old daughter, Rhea, from Leukemia.

Later in the workshop, Mike shared this:

"20 years ago, Trudy and I learned something that NO parent should ever have to discover: We learned how to bury a child. That's the wrong order of things. But we know how to do that now. I don't have a clue how to die, though. Will you all please help me?"

So vulnerable; so real. Honest.

Perhaps you have a group of peers in your life with which you can be that open and authentic? If so, you know how invaluable it can be as you seek to fulfill your purpose in life. We find our true identity, who we are meant to be, in community with others. So, if you're flying solo through life, I encourage you to find, or develop, a group of your own. The journey of life can be hard to navigate on your own.

Surround yourself with people who will tell you what you really need to hear, not just what you want to hear.

There's immeasurable value in having a cohort of people in your life that know you, love you, and want the best for you. Find a group you can go to and say:

"This is what I'm facing.
I don't know how to handle it.
Will you please help me?"

Many options are available: Business peer advisory boards; Faith community groups; Bible study groups; Life groups; Recovery groups; there are so many venues where you can become part of a community of like-minded people that will help you discover and become all you were meant to be.

Mike led such of group of like-minded CEOs. He was there for them. He invested himself in growing them. He helped them become all they were meant to be. In the end, they were there for him as well when he faced one of the most difficult chapters of his life.

Who are you serving this way? Who's there for you? Do you have such a community around you in life? If not, you might want to record an action to find, or cultivate, one for yourself.

Are you a Human *Being* – or a Human *Doing*?

Mike lived a full 15 months beyond his diagnosis. I stayed in touch with him after the workshop.

Each time we conversed, I learned something new and profound. In one conversation, he told me what his days were like with that terminal prognosis looming over him:

"I usually wake up very early – often before sunrise. I head to the kitchen and light a candle on the table. Trudy often joins me. We read together. We pray.

We talk, laugh, and sometimes cry. The other day she asked me what I wanted to do with the time I have left."

"What'd you say?" I eagerly asked.

"That's easy." Mike responded. *"Trudy … I just want to love you more!"*

Isn't that telling? Our priorities become acutely clear when we're faced with a very short amount of time. The thing Mike wanted more than anything was to make sure his wife, the love of his life, felt more deeply loved by him than ever before!

Mike had absolute clarity – his opportunity to tangibly express love to Trudy was drawing to a close. He didn't want to waste a single minute!

Beautiful!

Several weeks later I called Mike again:

"Mike! What are you up to these days?

"Well, I've been watching more movies since your workshop with my group."

'Excellent,' I thought to myself – *'I've created another movie fan in the world!'*

Before I could say that aloud, Mike continued:

"I love watching movies about Leadership. The other day I watched some film in which a US President was walking side-by-side with another world leader through the woods at Camp David. They were making world-changing leadership decisions as they walked side-by-side. As I watched the film, it occurred to me: Trudy and I aren't 'side-by-side' leaders."

"What do you mean?" I asked.

"We're back-to-back leaders!"

"You haven't helped," I confessed, a bit confused.

So, Mike continued:

"There's 180 degrees of things going on behind me that Trudy handles. I don't have a clue what she does, but she makes it all happen. There's 180 degrees of things going on behind Trudy I take care of that she knows nothing about – I just do it. It occurred to me the other morning: I'm not going to be here soon to light that candle. I need to make sure Trudy knows how to deal with all my stuff."

After I hung up, I reflected on the many conversations I'd had with my friend. I thought about who Mike was *being* in all my interactions with him – before, and after, his cancer diagnosis. Then, it hit me!

If we're truly living life in an extraordinary way, a shift will ultimately occur:

We'll stop drawing our identity from the things we DO in the world.

Our DOING in the world will start flowing from our IDENTITY. Who we ARE at our core. Our BEING.

I had this backwards in my head my whole life. I'd meet people on a plane. I'd introduce myself to them by telling them what I DID. It was as if I were a *Human Doing*. My *doing* defined who I was.

But as I considered the life of my friend, Mike Akers, my paradigm shifted. It did 'a 180°' of its own and turned completely around!

Before Mike led that group of CEOs as their mentor, he was a CEO himself. He was the kind of CEO you would have loved to work for. Why? Because he invested himself in his people – he worked hard to develop them as leaders – as humans.

Mike was a teacher at his core. That's who he was created to be. It was his *identity* – 'developing others' was his purpose in life. His teaching 'roles' and 'audiences' changed throughout life: teacher-students; father-kids; CEO-employees.

In his final days, Mike chose to invest some of his last hours in just me! In one-on-one phone calls, teaching me some profound life lessons!

Who are you at your core? What's *your* identity?

Not what you DO, but who were you created to BE?

Keep those questions in mind, and on your heart, as you continue reading this chapter.

The poem of your life

To set the stage for this part of our journey, we return briefly to 'The Welton Academy' – the college prep school for boys in the film, *Dead Poets' Society*.

In a scene called *Understanding Poetry*,[ii] Professor Keating, begins, energetically, to teach poetry.

Sweeping both arms towards himself in a broad, inviting motion, Keating gathers in his students around him. He bends down low in their midst like a coach in a sports team huddle. A hush falls over the room. The students stand in quiet expectation, anticipating a valuable life secret about to be proffered by their now beloved mentor.

Into the palpable silence, Professor Keating solemnly articulates this profound truth:

"We don't read and write poetry because it's cute. We read and write poetry because we are members of the human race. And the human race is filled with passion! Medicine, Law, Business, Engineering, these are noble pursuits ... necessary to sustain life. But Poetry, Beauty, Romance, Love ... these are what we stay alive for!"

Keating then quotes Whitman:

Oh me! Oh life!
Of the questions of these recurring;
Of the endless trains of the faithless — of cities fill'd with the foolish;
What good amid these, O me, O life?

Answer.

*That you are here — that life exists, and **identity**;*
That the powerful play goes on, and you may contribute a verse.

Keating slowly repeats the last line for emphasis:

> *That the powerful play goes on,*
> *and you may contribute a verse.*

He stresses each key word to ensure the message soaks into the ears of his captivated audience. The impact of those words visibly registers on the young men's faces — nods of affirmation, smiles of hope all around.

Keating then looks directly at shy, introverted young Mr. Anderson. He closes the lesson with the most philosophical question of the entire film:

"What will your verse be?"

Young Todd Anderson's inquisitive face is the last thing we see through the lens of the camera. The boy senses there is something here for him, but he's just not sure what it could be. We, the audience, *feel* the weight that question poses for this character we're slowly getting to know.

But more than that: we *feel* the impact those words pose for ourselves. We ponder *the poem of our own life*:

What will my verse be?

The drama again becomes personal for us. The scene fades to black.

Who are we as human beings?

Man has been exploring the essence of our existence from time immemorial. Renowned ancient Greek philosophers postulated about the various parts of our being. They concluded we are four-dimensional:

Body – Sóma (so'-mah) **Soul** – Psuché (psoo-khay')

Mind – Dianoia (dee-an'-oy-ah) **Spirit** - Pneuma (pnyoo'-mah)

Modern-day psychologists and psychiatrists have added to the 'what it means to be human' ideology. In the mid-20th century, based largely on the earlier work of Carl Rogers and Abraham Maslow, humanistic psychology rose to prominence. This view was less concerned with the parts of our nature and more concerned with our *whole being*.

We are greater than the sum of our parts.

We are, of course, *physical* beings. We have physical bodies. We live in physical world. We have physical needs and desires. However, those physical things don't define us completely as humans.

We are also *intellectual* beings. Our minds are capable of thought.

The human mind is so advanced that we can find ourselves thinking as we think. We can be aware of our awareness in any given moment. This ability to 'meta-cognate' makes us uniquely human. No other species can do that! Our minds are truly amazing in so many ways.

Each passing year, we learn new things about our minds thanks to the rapidly accelerating field of modern-day brain science. These two parts of our nature are spectacular! Yet, they fail to define us completely as humans. They can't because we are also *emotional* beings.

We have *souls* that can feel. We feel an incredibly wide range of emotions: love, anger, inspiration, depression, joy, sorrow, melancholy, rage, elation, and so many more! Yet, does adding this third, *emotional*, dimension of our nature define us completely as human beings? Perhaps something is still missing?

Consider an historical person to explore that possibility:

This particular leader was operating in a decades-long period of economic depression. Every measure of health, welfare, and prosperity was bad and getting worse. Industrial Production had been cut in half. Unemployment was skyrocketing. Corruption was rampant. Malnutrition and starvation were on the rise. Average life expectancy dropped precipitously as infant mortality and death by suicide increased dramatically. Got the picture? These were bad times!

Onto the stage stepped a leader. Brilliant. *Intellectual.* This leader envisioned new industries, producing *physical* products that the world needed, wanted, and were willing to pay for handsomely. He created over five million jobs and people throughout the nation returned to work, earning paychecks once again.

In just three years, industry expanded as much as it had during the preceding fifty years. Soon, every measure of economic wealth, health, and happiness turned around. This leader was making a huge difference in the world!

Talk about *emotional* ... no one was more passionate! This leader would bring crowds to their feet with his rousing speeches – speeches so inspired that audiences worked themselves up into frenzies! His fiery words and compelling rhetoric connected with them at a deep level. They were willing to go in whatever direction he encouraged.

By now you've probably figured it out.

I am, of course, describing: Adolf Hitler[iii].

Good leader? Great leader? Some people might say 'Yes.' Hitler moved people like few before and even fewer ever since. If a leader's greatness is measured only by how effectively they influence those around them, then 'yes' – he was a tremendously effective leader. No one else could have effected the kind of change in the world this man delivered.

But what was missing from how Hitler led – from his leadership *being*? Conscience? Compassion? Kindness? A well-calibrated moral compass perhaps?

Did Hitler ever once consider this question: *Is it right* to exterminate an entire race of people? *Is that a good thing?* He probably did. He wouldn't have called it *The Final Solution* if he didn't think it was *a good thing* to do. So yes, Hitler likely asked himself that very question.

But, consider this: *Was it right? Was it a good thing?* No need to pause to come up with the correct answer to this question!

It's easy, of course, to get confused in today's all too politically-correct culture in which we can't call something, or someone, 'wrong.' Today, it seems there's nothing really ever absolutely 'right' or 'wrong.' We can rationalize anything to ourselves or come up with some kind of a euphemism like: Well, maybe it was *right for him*. It was *his truth*.

Who are we to judge?

What? NO! By all means: NO! It was absolutely wrong!

Genocide is wrong. Always.

The man, and his political machine, consulted their *consciences*, individually and collectively, and got *a wrong answer* to a moral question.

How does that happen?

The very thought that it *can* happen, c*ould happen, to you or to me*, is completely terrifying!

The 18th century German Philosopher, Immanuel Kant, once notably said:

> *"Two things fill the mind with ever new and*
> *increasing admiration and awe:*
> *the starry heavens above me and*
> *the moral law within me."*

It's true: natural moral law is within us! There is an innate sense of right and wrong hardwired into the *conscience* of every human. To argue otherwise is to deny the *spiritual* part of your very nature.

You'll get a complete picture of who you are as a human being, your identity, only when you collectively consider all four parts of your being: Body, Mind, Soul, and Spirit.

Your Identity: Who you were created to be

In his critically-acclaimed sequel to *The Seven Habits of Highly Effective People,*[iv] titled *The Eighth Habit,*[v] Stephen Covey gives this concept of *Identity* another, delightful, name. He calls it your *'Voice'* and similarly asserts its position at the *overlapping intersection* of the four parts of your human nature.

Someone else we know calls it the same name!

In yet another scene[ii] from *Dead Poets' Society*, Professor Keating jumps up onto his desk at the front of the classroom. He encourages his students to do the same, one at a time. As the boys take their separate turns atop the desk, Keating exhorts them to *"find their own voice"* and not wait, lest they *"not find it at all!"*

The boys continue parading up onto the desk. One at a time, they hop up and then jump back down. Quietly, in the background, we hear the old familiar grandfather clock, this time, not ticking. Instead, we hear its deep chime, as hammer strikes the bell three times. Each time, it resounds with a low, rich, rhythmic: "Dong" ... "Dong" ... "Dong."

Time is marching on.

Closed briefcase now in hand, Keating walks deliberately towards the door at the back of the classroom. The end of class bell rings loudly as the final few boys make their way up and off the desk.

From the back of the room, Keating instructs them, for homework, to compose a poem of their own – *"an original work."*

Immediately, groans of agony emanate from the boys at the thought of writing their own poem. Undeterred, Keating literally taunts the boys with the assignment as he arrives at the exit door.

He flicks the lights on and off for dramatic effect as he announces they must speak it:

"Aloud. In front of the class, on Monday."

Keating steps out the door as the final two boys complete their trips up and off the desk. Suddenly, he pops back into the room as the last young man, Mr. Anderson, steps up onto the desk. Keating thunders Anderson's name.

Startled at the loud call of his name by his teacher, Anderson pauses mid-step atop the desk. He slightly regains his balance as Keating acknowledges aloud that he's fully aware this assignment terrifies the boy.

With that concluding goad, Keating turns off the classroom lights and leaves young Mr. Anderson alone on the desk … in the dark.

We see a look of utter dismay on the introverted young man's face. He awkwardly hops down to the floor amid some nervous laughter from the other boys.

We *feel* Mr. Anderson's misery with him as we too consider the prospect of finding and sharing our voice with the world around us.

The scene fades to black.

Walt Whitman, Stephen Covey, Professor Keating, and I all agree:

> *The poem of life goes on!*
> *You must strive to find your own voice; your identity;*
> *Your purpose; your Extraordinary Why; so that*
> *You can contribute your unique verse to the powerful*
> *play!*

Throughout this book, I'm pushing you out of your comfort zone to find *Your Extraordinary Why – your purpose.*

Here's a huge clue: it will most assuredly flow out of your *being –* your *Identity.* No one else on earth has the same unique combination of *physical* abilities, *intellectual* capabilities, *emotional* capacities, and *spiritual* sensitivities as you!

Without a doubt: "you are fearfully and wonderfully made."[vii]

You're already well on the journey of discovery – great!

But remember, time is of the essence:

In the next chapter, we'll take a further step to explore the crucial role your *spiritual* being plays in connecting you to your true purpose. Before we do, let's more deeply consider that earlier, troubling question:

How can our conscience give us a <u>wrong</u> answer to a moral question?

Take a moment to consider how that can happen.

Your relationship with your conscience

Think of your conscience as if it's a muscle. Each day, it prompts you – it woos you to come to the gym and work out with it. If we obey, and yield to, the promptings of our conscience, that's what we do: We go to the gym and work it out. In the process, our conscience gets a little bit stronger as a result.

It's not always comfortable to follow those promptings. Sometimes, obeying our conscience requires us to take actions contrary to our desires.

Often, those promptings require us to wage war on our one of our fiercest foes – our ego:

- We're prompted to apologize for an unkind word or action.
- We're urged to own a personal misstep.
- Overlook an offense.
- Seek forgiveness.

Sometimes, obedience to the urgings of our conscience requires us to take a risk – something we wouldn't normally do. We may be quiet by nature and our conscience speaks clearly to us, urging us to be vocal about a situation: a wrong we've witnessed or an injustice in our midst.

Doing so can be emotional for us. Scary. Awkward. But we *know* it's the right thing to do.

Yes, obeying the promptings of our conscience can be uncomfortable. But the best workouts always are uncomfortable!

When we physically work out, we wage war on the inactivity that leads to the breakdown of our muscles. The workout is not comfortable. We stress and strain those muscles as we put them through the paces. We literally create micro-tears in the muscle fibers during the workout. Yet, it is in the recovery from that workout that our muscles ultimately growth stronger. Tears heal and the tissue becomes more resilient.

Working out is a choice, however. We don't *have* to do it. We can choose instead to skip the workout. To ignore the promptings of our conscience: we can *know* the right thing to do but still choose *not* to do it.

That's like staying home on the couch, binge-watching Netflix on TV, skipping the workout. That's certainly more comfortable! But our muscles weaken as a result of our choice. If we keep on ignoring those promptings, the muscle of our conscience begins to atrophy from lack of use. We become less sensitive to its urgings. What used to trouble us no longer seems to irritate or agitate as it once did.

Ignore our conscience beyond the point of atrophy and we can wound it further still. We can sear it or numb it entirely. Our conscience will never bother us again.

We will have become amoral.

amoral
[ey-**mawr**-*uh*]]

Adjective

- not involving questions of right or wrong; without moral quality; neither moral not immoral; having no moral standards, restraints, or principles; unaware of or indifferent to questions of right or wrong.

Gradually, the choices we make become progressive. They are self-affirming. Choosing to do three workouts this week makes it easier to make the same choice next week, then the next week, and so on. If we form the habit of working out, and exercise becomes our norm, we grow physically fit and our health improves. If we choose not to work out at all, we become progressively less fit and our health deteriorates.

Similarly, the choices we make responding to the promptings of our conscience are also progressive. Choosing to respond affirmatively to our conscience today makes it easier to do so tomorrow and the next day.

Over time, if we cultivate a habit of making conscience-centered choices, we become more spiritually fit. We become more aware. Eventually, our relationships with those around us improve as a result. Progressively, responses to our conscience's prompting accumulate.

Ultimately, our chosen responses to those promptings define the nature and quality of relationship we have with our conscience.

Your relationship with your conscience can serve as a reliable, well-calibrated guidance system — one that steers you rightly and serves the world well.

OR:

Your relationship with your conscience can become useless to you and potentially harmful to the world around you.

The choice is always yours!

*"No one knows what he himself is made of,
except his own spirit within him,
yet there is still some part of him which remains hidden,
even from his own spirit."*
— *Augustine*

NOTES

i. Vistage is the world's largest CEO development forum. Private Advisory Boards of non-competing business owners and CEOs meet monthly in a safe, confidential, environment to process issues and opportunities and help each other become better leaders who make better decisions, and get better results. More details can be found at www.vistage.com.

ii. "Understanding Poetry." *Dead Poet's Society*, directed by Peter Weir (1989; Los Angeles, CA: Touchstone Pictures, 1998), DVD.

iii. Mark Weber, "How Hitler Tackled Unemployment And Revived Germany's Economy," (Institute for Historical Review 2012): accessed October 4, 2019, http://www.ihr.org/other/economyhitler2011.html

iv. Stephen Covey, *7 Habits of Highly Effective People* (New York, NY: Simon & Schuster, Inc. 1989).

v. Stephen Covey, *The 8th Habit – From Effectiveness to Greatness* (New York, NY: Simon & Schuster, Inc. 2004).

vi. "A Different Perspective." *Dead Poet's Society*, directed by Peter Weir (1989; Burbank, CA: Warner Home Video, 1998), DVD.

vii. Psalm 139:14 Scripture taken from the HOLY BIBLE, NEW INTERNATIONAL VERSION® (NIV). Copyright © 1973, 1978, 1984 International Bible Society. Used by permission of Zondervan. All rights reserved.

Chapter 8

The Key to Unlocking Your True Purpose

> *"The powerful play goes on,*
> *and you may contribute a verse."*
> *— Walt Whitman*

Time is short.

You've got a lot to do and a limited amount of time to do it. But how do you decide where to invest your only limited resource? How will you know if the decisions you make today will lead you closer to, or farther from, *Your Desired Legacy?*

Traditional goal setting

So much has already been written about goal setting. It's universally accepted that those who make a habit of setting intentional goals achieve more than those that don't. *Proactive* people are more effective than reactive people.

Goals catalyze action in a specific direction. They signal intentionality. Goals illuminate choices and inform decisions.

No realm is more familiar with, and insistent upon, goal setting and performance than the commercial marketplace. Almost all effective organizations have structured goal setting processes. Planning is a regular part of running a business or any kind of ongoing venture.

What are we going to do? When are we going to do it? How are we going to get it done?

Long term strategic plans. Short term tactical plans. Annual, quarterly, monthly, weekly and daily plans are all a normal part of life in an organization.

Here's how traditional goal setting works in a typical organization:

- Start with focus on a particular measure: *Revenue.*
- Ask a question: *"How much will we sell next year?"*
- Analyze internal considerations:
  - Last year's revenue? Projected end of year revenue?
  - New business capacity without compromising effectiveness? New sales initiatives? Stakeholder expectations?
- Analyze external considerations:
  - Market for our product; what's our share of that market?
  - Is demand for our product growing or shrinking?
  - What is our competition doing? What's our response?
  - What disruptors could cause shifts in our business?
  - How's the overall economy? Will it affect our demand?

After analysis, Sales Leadership typically sets a goal: *"Next year, our goal is to sell $xx,xxx,xxx!"*

Sales team members, responsible for goal delivery, respond: *"There's no way! That's too high! It's not possible!"*

Internal 'negotiation' ensues.

Eventually, a Revenue Goal is set and agreed upon by those in Leadership and those responsible for delivering it.

You know the process – goal setting in a group is a complex, iterative, thing. Nonetheless, almost all organizations do it. Why?

Because it works! At the end of the goal-setting process, the organization has a powerful thing:

A written goal that's mutually shared within the organization

That goal spurs the organization into coordinated action. All individuals in the boat are rowing in the same direction toward the same destination.

The process is similar when individuals set goals. Here's how a typical *individual* sets goals:

- Start with focus on a particular measure: *Personal Weight.*
- Ask a question: *"By the end of next year, what do I want to weigh?"*
- Analyze internal considerations:
  - What is my current weight?
  - What did I weigh when I felt my best?
  - Given my height/body type, what weight is most healthy for me?
  - Am I really committed to make changes to achieve my ideal weight?
  - What do I already know about weight loss? What do I need to learn?
- Analyze external considerations:
  - What upcoming events will motivate me to lose weight?
  - What circumstances will hinder me from making necessary changes?
  - What's a realistic weight loss goal given my timeframe?

After we consider all that, we set a personal goal:

"By December 31st, I will have lost 25 pounds."

We write it down or perhaps share it with others for accountability. At the end of that personal goal setting process, we have something powerful:

A written personal goal, that we're committed to achieving.

That goal propels us towards positive action. The goal enables us to make the necessary daily adjustments to our lifestyle in order to achieve our goal weight.

Goals are very powerful things.

In both examples, consider which parts of *your being* were used to set those goals. The organization, and the individual, considered *physical need(s) or want(s)*:

Organizational Goal	Personal Goal
How much do we want to sell?	What do I weigh now?
How much does the market need?	What do I want to weigh in the future?
What do our stakeholders expect?	By when do I want achieve that ideal weight?

Then, they used their *intellectual mind(s)* to perform some analysis:

Organizational Goal	Personal Goal
What do we have the capability to deliver?	Is it reasonable to lose weight at that rate?
What strategies will we use to sell that much?	What circumstances might help or hinder me?
What must we do to effectively compete?	Who might help me achieve that goal?

After considering *physical* needs and wants, and performing some *intellectual* analysis, the goals were set. The goals then existed in the *minds* of the individuals involved and they were even *physically* written down. At that point, they became powerful things for the organization and the individual.

But notice this:

In both cases, the goals set were 'half-being' goals.

Only the *physical* and *intellectual* parts of being were engaged in the goal setting process. Only half of the whole being, individual or organization, was involved in the process!

Clearly, *half-being goals* have the power to motivate, drive change, and produce results. We know this to be true, for we see it work all the time in our organizations. We've also seen it work for us personally.

But … just imagine the power that flows from *whole-being goals*!

The power of *why*

Getting to *Why* evokes emotion. *Whys* inspire others and bring out their passion! Goals we set when we start with our *why* are especially motivating.

Here's an example: I mentioned earlier that I spent a large part of my corporate career working in the Oil and Gas Industry.

What did I do?

Well, large multinational integrated oil companies find large deposits of petroleum reserves deep under the earth; they extract them to the service; they distill and refine them into useful components; they deliver those products to market; then, they sell them to businesses and consumers. That's the *what* of the Oil and Gas business.

The world needs those products; the industry provides jobs; shareholders expect to make money – all noble worthy goals.

But that *what* doesn't exactly create fire in the belly! At least, it never really did for me. So, I always challenged the teams I led to get beyond the *what* of our business. I encouraged them to dig deep. To ask enough *why* questions to get to some motivators that inspired them.

Here were some answers they came up with over the years:

- We provide energy that keeps families warm.
- We help people cook food to feed themselves and their children.
- We provide fuel that gives people the mobility they need to get to their places of work and visit loved ones far away.
- We create chemicals that make Christmas tree lights heat resistant and safe so that people don't needlessly die in house fires.
- We help developing countries tap into their natural gas reserves so they can generate power from cleaner sources.

That final *why* was incredibly motivating to a team I encountered when living in Hong Kong.

In China, the air was so thick with fumes from coal-fired power plants that average people routinely wore masks just to ease the burden on their lungs. Once the people on this team became clear on *their why,* they stopped coming to work to "find, produce and sell natural gas and power."

That was *what* they did, but they worked tirelessly, exerting full effort to give their aging parents and young children cleaner air to breathe! Warmth, Food, Mobility, Safety, Power, and Clean Air!

Those *whys* are *poetry*, motivating and inspiring! They give us a reason to get up each morning – to work hard and give our all because we are making a positive difference in the world.

Those *whys* fire us up or choke us up! They tap into our emotional soul and bring out our best.

So, while typical *physical* and *intellectual* goal setting is effective, adding the *emotional* element of *why* into the process is even more so!

That's why I pushed you earlier in the book to find some big *whys* in your life that drive you. There's power for you in those *whys*!

A more reflective approach to goal setting

Consider the possibility of an even more powerful approach to goal setting – more powerful than typical physical & intellectual goal setting. More powerful than even adding the emotion of *why* into the process.

I call it *Conscience-Centered Goal Setting.* It's a simple five-step process that works like this:

Step 1: Create solitude

Get alone in a space where you can be uninterrupted, undistracted.

Turn off cell phones, TVs, radios, and other noise making devices.

Settle comfortably into this quiet place.

Bring only yourself and a journal.

Step 2: Quiet your mind

For typical goal setting, we begin by asking our *mind* a question. In *Conscience-Centered Goal Setting,* however, we begin by quieting our minds. If silencing your mind causes you stress, don't panic! We'll engage that part of our being later. Just not at the outset.

This step can take some time, especially in today's hectic world, where our minds are energized and active. To effectively engage with our conscience, we must temporarily get our minds out of the way. Be patient.

Keeping a journal, or the *Extraordinary Why Companion Workbook,* nearby will help. Alone in your quiet place, as *thoughts* come to *mind,* don't be disturbed by them. Just jot them down on a page labeled 'Thoughts to Consider Later.' As a thought occurs, write just a word or two. Then, thank your mind for sharing the thought. Seriously! Your mind is powerful! It's there to help you. If you acknowledge its contribution, it will become still, allowing you to return to your practice of giving it some much-needed rest.

Breathe deeply as you go through this process. Our brains need oxygen to function. When we're stressed, often our breathing gets shallow and more rapid, causing our stress to build even further. By slowing down and taking deep breaths, we send a signal to our brain that 'all is well.' It can rest from processing for a while – we are safe.

Some call this practice of quieting your mind *meditation*. Others call it *centering prayer*. Others don't call it anything at all. It's not important to give the practice a name. But it *is* important to do it if you want to tap into the most creative, reflective, and powerful part of your being – your Spirit!

Quieting your mind may not come easily. Don't give up. Persist in the task of stilling your thoughts to connect more deeply to who you are at your core – your Identity: who you were created to be. Again, be patient with yourself. The more you practice this, the easier it will become for you.

Step 3: Ask your *conscience* a question. Be silent.

That's right. Ask your *conscience* – NOT your *mind*. We're so practiced at interacting with our mind – the intellectual part of our being – that this activity can seem unfamiliar at first. You may not have engaged it in proactive conversation for a while.

Relax.

You do *know* the voice of your conscience. It's been with you your whole life. So even if it seems unfamiliar to you now, relax and take some time to get reacquainted.

Some people think of their conscience as a *'still small voice'* at the back of their mind, coaching, counseling, advising in the way they should go or what they should, or shouldn't, do. Others, with a tradition of faith, think of their conscience as *'the Voice of God'* speaking to them – the Creator of their very being speaking directly to its creature.

Still others may view it in an entirely different way altogether.

In any of these cases, however, most people seem to have a first-person/third-party relationship with their conscience – as if it's part of them, yet also separate from them.

This is the part of your being that you're engaging with during *conscience-centered* conversations.

Some suggestions for engaging with your conscience:

- Ask it big questions. Deep questions.
- Remain quiet. Be silent.
- Listen in the silence.
- Be patient with yourself.

Step 4: Be present with emotions. Remain Silent. Journal.

You will *know* when you've heard back from your conscience. How? You'll likely get *emotional.* You may get fired up. You may get choked up. You may feel encouraged by its voice. You may feel convicted by its offering to you. It'll be different for all of us, at different times, but this seems universally true:

When you ask your conscience a question, it __will__ respond.
You will __know__, at the core of your being,
that you've heard.
You'll have an emotional response.

It may be a powerful, profound feeling or it may not be so dramatic. Either way, as you experience an emotional response to what you hear, sit with that emotion for a while. Allow yourself to *feel* it.

Now, reengage your conscience once again around that emotion. Ask it *why* you're feeling emotional? Where is that emotion coming from? Why do you feel it as intensely as you do?

Eventually, during this process, your mind will inevitably reengage.

Sometimes, your mind's offerings may not be helpful. Perhaps it will discourage you from continuing: "This is a waste of time." If you hear such things, acknowledge them. Respond back: "thank you for sharing." Once acknowledged, your mind will usually quiet down — then you can reengage in the process of discerning the voice of your conscience.

Eventually, your mind will hear and acknowledge the promptings of your conscience. Your mind will help you process the emotions you're experiencing. Then it will do an amazing thing for you: Your mind will activate your hand. You'll begin writing! Jot down whatever you hear at that point into your journal on a page labeled: *'Responses from my Conscience.'*

Step 5: Ask clarifying questions. Keep journaling.

Often, people find it useful to ask clarifying questions. It's easy to be satisfied with initial revelations you receive from engaging in *conscience-centered goal setting*. However, it's wise to remain in the moment. It took time and effort to get to the place where you were able to hear clearly from your conscience. Don't rush out of it! Stay in the moment. Repeat the process, once or several times, with related follow-up questions.

Once again, ask these questions of your conscience, not your mind. Questions like: "I sense I'm hearing this from you. Am I getting that right? Hearing you clearly?" What else do you want me to know?"

Get silent after each clarifying question. Keep writing down the responses you receive. They may not make sense to you initially. Don't be concerned with that.

Eventually, the responses will come together for you as you continue to reflect on them.

Conscience-Centered Goal Setting in Summary

Here it is in summary – a simple, five-step process:

Conscience-Centered Goal Setting

1 – Create solitude
2 – Quiet your mind
3 – Ask your conscience a question. Be silent.
4 – Be present with emotions. Remain silent. Journal.
5 – Ask clarifying questions. Keep journaling.

Typical goal-setting processes are powerful. They deliver written goals that drive performance. They lead to success. That's why so many people and so many organizations set goals; they work and they lead to success.

But typical goal setting processes deliver "half-being goals." They are the product of a process that engaged only your mind and the physical part of your being – only half of your being.

At the end of *conscience-centered goal setting*, however, notice what you have: *Whole-being goals!*

Whole Being Goals

Birthed from your conscience,
Moved through your emotions,
Processed by your intellect, and
Recorded by your physical being.

Whole-being goals possess the power to transform! Inevitably, their achievement leads to significance!

Practicing *Conscience-Centered Goal Setting*

Ready to give it a try?

The *Extraordinary Why Companion Workbook* is filled with conscience-based questions that will give you plenty of practice. For now, let's start with a single question that will help you further clarify *Your Desired Legacy*.

Grab a journal and something with which to write.

Create solitude in a quiet, distraction-free place.

Now, ask your conscience this question:

Before I leave planet earth, what must I do?

Remember, you're not asking your mind this question. You're asking your *conscience*.

If you immediately start writing down answers to that question, chances are it was your mind speaking through your pen, not your conscience. If that happens, just relax. Thank your mind for sharing and continue getting more deeply in touch with your conscience.

Take your time with this exercise. When writing, don't worry about getting it perfect. Wait until you get emotional about something and just write what you hear – whether or not it makes sense to you initially.

Be patient with yourself as you go through this process. There's no need to rush.

Your Extraordinary Why Journal

What must I do before I leave planet earth?

Responses From My Conscience

_____
_____
_____
_____
_____
_____
_____
_____
_____
_____
_____
_____
_____
_____
_____
_____

Now ask clarifying questions like the following and keep on journaling:

"Am I hearing you clearly?"   *"What else do I need to know?"*

_____
_____
_____
_____
_____
_____
_____
_____

Having gotten this far, take a deep breath. Remain in this reflective space for just a little longer.

Look at the responses you just received from your conscience, and respond to these following additional questions:

Did you write down a goal that particularly resonates with you? If so, summarize it, succinctly, in the space below:

_____
_____
_____
_____
_____

Now answer this: *Why* is that goal important to you?

_____
_____
_____
_____

Now dig just a bit deeper: *Why* is *that* important to you?

_____
_____
_____
_____

Conscience is the key

Did you experience a greater degree of clarity by digging for a deeper why behind the goal your conscience prompted you with in that exercise? The why behind your why?

If not, you may want to drill down into that why another time or two until you reach something truly meaningful for you. When you do, you'll likely encounter something profound.

If you dig deep enough into this practice, invariably you'll come face-to-face with something related to your identity:

> *Who you are at the core of your being.*
> *Who you were created to be.*
> *Your Extraordinary Why.*
> *Your Purpose.*

Here are answers I often hear from my workshop participants:

- "I must accomplish this goal because it's why I'm here."

- "When I have accomplished it, I will have achieved something significant."

- "This is something that truly matters."

- "In the end, it's the *only* thing that really matters!"

- "This goal is bigger than me. It will be of lasting benefit to those in the world after I'm gone."

- "If I don't get this done, I will have wasted my life."

- "I know this is my life's calling."

- "Achieving this goal will define my legacy!"

When we speak phrases like these, we have clearly gotten in touch with our purpose. That's the all-important secret to, and power in, this kind of reflective, iterative, practice of *Conscience-Centered Goal Setting.*

> *Your conscience is the key*
> *that unlocks the door*
> *to your purpose!*

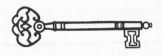

Remember Walt Whitman's poem?

O me! O Life!

Oh me! Oh life! … of the questions of these recurring;
Of the endless trains of the faithless – of cities fill'd with the foolish;
What good amid these, O me, O life?

Answer.

That you are here – that life exists, and identity;
That the powerful play goes on, and you may contribute a verse.

The whole poem wonderfully reflects a *conscience-centered conversation*.

First, Whitman asks himself a question:

Oh me! Oh life! … of the questions of these recurring;
Of the endless trains of the faithless – of cities fill'd with the foolish;
What good amid these, O me, O life?

That's a great question. A big question! No doubt, a long period of silence followed that great question.

I'm sure even Whitman experienced a few distracting thoughts as he held that question out before himself, repeating it to himself over and over as he meditated upon it:

"What good amid these, O me, O life?"

Eventually, Whitman heard from his conscience. He got a clear answer to the question he was being present with in the silence.
He even labeled it so!

Answer.
*That you are here – that life exists, **and identity;***
*That the powerful play goes on, and **you may contribute a verse.***

That answer was directly related to his identity – who he was at his core. Whitman was a poet!

His purpose – *to contribute a verse to the powerful play of life* – flowed out of identity as a poet. Whitman got his answer as he wrestled long and hard with this conscience in the conversation that birthed that poem.

What a beautiful example – a lesson to us all!

The question remains for you:

What will your verse be?

You will only find the answer to that question when you engage in deep reflective conversations with your conscience. For it is your conscience, with whom you have that almost mystical, first-person/third-party, relationship, that is the key to the door that gets you beyond yourself.

> *Only your conscience will lead you to the purpose you were created to fulfill while you are here on earth.*

In his landmark book, *The Purpose Driven Life: What on Earth am I Here for?,*[i] author Rick Warren wrote:

> *"The search for the purpose of life has puzzled people for thousands of years. That's because we typically begin at the wrong starting point – ourselves. We ask self-centered questions like What do I want to be? What should I do with my life? What are my goals, my ambitions, my dreams for my future? But focusing on ourselves will never reveal our life's purpose."*

If we ask ourselves such questions with just a portion of our being, we'll never grasp the fullness of the answer that's waiting for us.

Our *physical* being is incapable of answering a meta-physical question. Our *intellect* alone cannot deliver a satisfactory answer for it is consumed with only tangible facts and perceived realities. Our *emotions* can deceive us and take us down paths we were never intended to wander.

It is your conscience, that *spiritual* part of your being, that nudges you out of yourself and in touch with your Creator – the source that created you for a specific purpose. Your conscience, that fourth part of your being, gives life to your *voice*. Your conscience will give you access to that verse you must contribute to 'the powerful play' of life as you fulfill your purpose.

Why wait any longer to incorporate this powerful practice of *Conscience Centered Goal Setting* into your life?

Remember, time is marching on:

"Being successful and fulfilling
your life's purpose
are not at all the same issue!
You could reach all your personal goals,
becoming a raving success by the world's standard
and still miss [your purpose in life.]"
– Rick Warren

NOTES

i. Rick Warren, *The Purpose Driven Life: What on Earth Am I Here For?* Expanded Ed. (Zondervan, Copyright © 2002, 2011, 2012). Used by permission of Zondervan. All rights reserved.

Chapter 9

Living From Your Extraordinary Why

"Every man dies. Not every man really lives!"
— William Wallace

In the last chapter, you learned and practiced *Conscience-Centered Goal Setting* – a contemplative approach to setting meaningful goals that engages your *whole being*.

Now, you'll have the opportunity to apply that practice to further illuminate and refine *Your Extraordinary Why*.

I'll also introduce you to an incredibly powerful tool that enables you to take charge of your legacy and create your desired future *from* your future.

Conscience-Centered Goal Setting from *Your Extraordinary Why*

Your Extraordinary Why holds deep meaning for you. It is your *Life Purpose* – your ultimate *Yonder Star*. Knowing your purpose empowers you to prioritize your life around the projects, people, and relationships that mean the most to you.

You can then set goals and create life habits that align with those priorities. You can say *yes* to things that align with your purpose and say *no* to other things that distract.

In so doing, you begin to *live from Your Extraordinary Why*.

For example, because my wife Jeanne is the most important person in my life, I place a high priority on nurturing the health of our marriage. We've made a habit of reminding ourselves of the commitment we made the day we married.

Each week, sometime every Sunday for now almost 30 years, we find a time to repeat our wedding vows to each other. Some weeks it's very easy to do – other weeks it can be more difficult. But regardless of the kind of week we've had together, we reaffirm and remind ourselves of the commitment we made back in November of 1990, and *why* we made it. It's a ritual that has served our family very well.

Similarly, another of my most important goals in life is to have *a unique, deep and abiding relationship with each one of my children.* In support of that goal I took each of my kids on a one-on-one trip while they were in their teenage years. To help them develop their own relationship with their conscience, I asked them to set the agenda – where we would go and what we would do. It wasn't *my* trip where *they* tagged along, but it was *their* trip where *I* joined them.

My oldest daughter, Lauren, decided she wanted to help an orphanage in the inner-city slums of Santo Domingo in the Dominican Republic. It was NOT the kind of trip I would have picked, nor was it luxurious in the least! But we learned so much about ourselves and about each other as we traveled.

When the plane touched down on the tarmac in Santa Domingo that summer day, it didn't exactly occur to us that we were literally leaving behind *'comfort.'* Electricity, clean running water, air conditioning – all that was back on the plane. When we stepped out into the jet bridge and progressed through the airport, we left it all behind. I had never experienced poverty first-hand until that moment of my life.

I knew I should be filled with gratitude for that fact. But, bottom line: I was simply too uncomfortable in the moment to appreciate my overall blessed life.

The first night there was long. The heat and humidity were oppressive. The crowded room I shared with three other men was so stuffy we had to keep the one small window open to get air. This, of course, let in the loud city noises since we were right in the heart of town. The little sleep I managed was fitful at best. I woke early the next morning dripping in sweat, covered with mosquito bites on top of my bed bug bites ... ugh!

I bumped into Lauren alone in the hall before anyone else was stirring. She looked at me with eyes filled with tears and said:

"Oh Daddy ... I want to go home!"

"I know, babe. Me too!" I replied. *"We will go home. I promise. In about eight days when our plane comes back."*

After a brief pause, I couldn't help myself. Drolly, I added:

"I sure wish you would've picked someplace cooler!"

Lauren grimaced at my tongue-in-cheek, though not-so-subtle, reminder that we were there by choice – HER choice. I smiled broadly and pulled her close to give her a reassuring hug – we were in this together!

That afternoon our group went to Jackie's House – the orphanage where we'd be doing some of our mission work. It was set in a beautiful rural area on the outskirts of Santo Domingo. While it was still oppressively hot, the peaceful setting was a stark contrast to the bustling center of the city.

Jackie immediately impressed me when she walked out to meet our group. Kids, of course, surrounded her. A small one was in her arms. Two others were wrapped around her legs. That didn't surprise me. We were in an orphanage where children were hungry for love and affection – not just food.

What I did not expect, however, was to see such a beautiful, serene woman. Jackie's countenance glowed. She radiated! Outwardly, yes, but also from an inner beauty that was immediately apparent.

As we chatted that day, Jackie spoke effusively about her faith. She told me about some of the two-way conversations she regularly had with God and about how much He loved her. It was so refreshing to hear. This was a woman truly living from her *Extraordinary Why*.

Later that evening, I asked my conscience to reveal what exactly I had seen in Jackie's countenance that afternoon. Quietly, but most assuredly, I received my answer:

'It's the kind of beauty that comes only from love.'

Immediately, that revelation resonated deeply with my soul. Jackie knew she was so loved by her Creator, and His love overflowed out of her into the orphanage kids. It was her intimate knowledge of God's love for her that caused Jackie's countenance to glow!

I asked my conscience what I should do with that revelation, and I waited in silence. My conscience began speaking.

It spoke even more until I became emotional. As my mind processed all the emotions, I began to think about my wife, Jeanne. Soon, these words came out in my journal:

'I want Jeanne's countenance to glow —
To radiate from an inner source of knowledge
and deeply felt emotion that she is loved by me.
Not for anything she does,
but just for who God created her to be.'

That's *True North* for me on the compass that guides me in my relationship with my wife. On my best days, it directs my attitudes, behaviors, choices, and decisions when I interact with her. I've learned that some of my *ABCDs* can cause Jeanne to 'glow' more brightly, while others can have the opposite effect. For Jeanne, that's my *Yonder Star – Desired Legacy*.

In what will surely be remembered as one of the most profound pictures of 2019, *A Beautiful Day in the Neighborhood,*[i] Tom Hanks delightfully portrays Fred Rogers, the beloved children's television program host, and star, of *Mister Rogers*. In the film we meet Lloyd Vogel (Matthew Rhys), a writer working for *Esquire* magazine. He is tasked with delivering a story on Fred Rogers for an upcoming edition.

In the opening scene we learn that Lloyd carries a lot of anger with him and has to learn about *forgiveness*.

Further into the movie, at just the right moment in Lloyd's life story, Mr. Rogers takes him to lunch. During the conversation, Fred tells Lloyd to take just one minute of silence to "think of all the people *who loved him into being*."

Then, in some of the most moving 60 seconds in the history of film, Mr. Rogers looks out at us, the audience, inviting us to join Lloyd in that simple exercise. Time stands still in those moments of silence as we all embark on our own trip down memory lane. It's powerful!

Why not invest just 60 seconds of silence, right now, to take that journey for yourself?

Who loved you into being?

Don't rush. Take a full minute to reflect on that simple, deep question.

Now that you've finished meditating on that penetrating question, write down your responses to the following questions:

- **Who loved** *you* **into** *being*?

- **How connected are you to your Creator's love for you?**

- **What** *love* **goals do you want to set right now –**

    o **For yourself?**

    o **For those people that mean the most to you?**

    o **For others in the world around you?**

As the character *"Love,"* beautifully played by Keira Knightly in the movie <u>*Collateral Beauty*</u>,[ii] said so eloquently:

"I am the reason for everything.
I am <u>the only</u> Why.
Please don't try to live without me."

This journey of *Life* really is all about *Love!*

Conscience, Love, and *Your Extraordinary Why*

While reflecting on the *Love* in your life – past, present, and future – take a few moments now to invite your conscience to further illuminate *Your Extraordinary Why*.

Don't overthink this. You've invested yourself in this journey we've been traveling. You've connected deeply with your conscience. You've reflected on the big questions of life. You've perhaps never been more prepared for this exercise – so don't hesitate now.

Slowly, one at a time, ask yourself the following questions.

Wait for the emotions. They will be your sign that your conscience is speaking to you.

Allow your intellect to process those emotions.

Write down the answers that come to you after your *mind* processes the *emotions* that your *conscience* prompts in response to these questions:

What must I do before I leave planet Earth?

_____
_____
_____
_____
_____

Why does that matter?

_____
_____
_____
_____
_____

Why does THAT matter?

_____

_____

_____

_____

_____

Why am I here on planet Earth?

_____

_____

_____

_____

Now, reread all your responses.

Focus on what you wrote after that last question:

'Why am I here on planet Earth?'

On the next page, make any adjustments to summarize that answer into a simple expression of *Your Extraordinary Why.*

My Extraordinary Why:

_____

_____

_____

_____

_____

_____

_____

_____

_____

_____

_____

_____

_____

_____

_____

_____

Good for you ... there it is!

It might be helpful to sign and date this page. Years from now, you may return to this. Think how meaningful it will be for you *then* to look back and reflect on what you just wrote at this particular date and time! Take a moment to do that now, below:

Dear Future Self,

On, this date, _____, I hereby declared the above to be my Extraordinary Why – my purpose in life.

Signed: _____

Taking charge of your legacy

With *Your Extraordinary Why* now clearly in your mind, it's time to take charge of creating your legacy like never before. I'll introduce you to a powerful tool that will help you do just that, but first a bit of drama to set the stage!

This time, however, we won't turn to the *'Silver Screen'* of Hollywood for inspiration. This time we'll get some help from the dazzling *'Lights of Broadway!'*

In 2016, <u>*Hamilton: An American Musical*</u>[iii] took Broadway and the world by storm! The original production earned 16 Tony Award nominations and won 11 Tony Awards (including *Best Musical*). It also earned the Pulitzer Prize for *Drama* that year.

To say there's a hit song in the smash Broadway sensation would be an understatement. The musical's accolades also include 2016's Grammy Award for *Best Musical Theater Album*.

The 46-track album has broken Broadway album sales records and has earned universal praise from fans and critics alike.

In the musical's main theme, *"My Shot"*[iv] we learn that our protagonist, Alexander Hamilton, is particularly keen to secure his legacy in the hearts and minds of generations yet to come.

In the song, Hamilton raps:

"Don't be shocked when your history book mentions me
I will lay down my life if it sets us free
Eventually you'll see my ascendancy
I'm not throwing away my shot!"

Talk about a man fixated on securing his *Desired Legacy.* Hamilton is *driven* to make his life count! His egocentric motives are also clear:

Hamilton wants to be remembered and adored by the world for his accomplishments.

Later in the play, a wise, aging George Washington offers fatherly advice to the younger, enthusiastic Hamilton. Washington counsels Hamilton that we don't get to decide who ultimately tells our story or even what that story will be – your final legacy is somewhat beyond your control, Washington asserts. Nonetheless, be intentional about creating your legacy because:

"History Has Its Eyes On You"

Sage advice from our Founding Father and first President – History *is* watching you. Its eyes *are* on you. You *are* indeed leaving a legacy.

But is it *completely* out of your control?

Hamilton seems unconvinced. He raps on that in his imagination, his inevitable death is so real to him that it feels more like a past memory than a future event. In his mind, Hamilton is not bound by time. Throughout this wonderful production that really is all about *Legacy*, Hamilton keeps repeating the refrain:

"I'm not throwing away my shot!"

If you've experienced the musical, or have listened to the soundtrack, you probably even hear that line resonating in your mind right now, too – it's such a catchy tune!

For whatever the reason, Hamilton is committed to *living his life from the legacy* he wants to create.

He is: ***Working really hard at becoming a good ancestor.***

How about you?

I suspect you too are working to become the best possible ancestor for your descendants, or you wouldn't still be reading! So, as we near the end of our time together, I'll share with you a powerful tool you can use to take charge of your legacy like never before.

Creating your legacy *from* your legacy

In an article called, *"The Merlin Exercise: Future by Forecast or Future by Invention,"* authors R.M. Fulmer and S. Perret describe a powerful future-first planning method. It's been used in many corporate settings for strategic planning and project planning purposes.

The concept is that since it's difficult to create a new, transformed, reality while living in the existing reality – don't even try. Rather, create the breakthrough future you desire *from* the future.

According to legend, Merlin the magician was mentor and advisor to King Arthur. As described in T.H. White's *The Once and Future King*[vii], Merlin had an uncanny ability to know the future because he was:

"... born at the wrong end of time." Merlin was *"forced to live backwards in time from the future while surrounded by people living forward from behind!"*

Following Merlin's lead, don't work *towards* your *Desired Legacy* – rather:

> *Envision your Desired Legacy as already achieved!*
> *Then, work your way backwards from it.*

In the next few pages, you'll have the opportunity to apply Merlin's magical powers for yourself. You'll take charge of your legacy and create it backwards from having already achieved it!

"Merlin" Your Legacy

Get silent and take a few deep, cleansing breaths.

Now, in your mind's eye, picture yourself well out into the future.

Apply *Conscience-Centered Goal Setting* and begin journaling as you ask your conscience:

> *What does the world around me look like now that I have achieved my desired legacy?*

Silently reflect on that question.

Don't start writing immediately. Wait for your emotions to kick in as a sign that you've connected deeply with your conscience.

Once they do, begin journaling, in the present tense. How do you *feel* about *yourself;* your *family; your community* now that you have accomplished your desired legacy?

Whom do you now know *yourself* to be, having achieved your goal? What is now possible for your descendants, and others, that wasn't even remotely feasible before you lived your life?

Write it all out in as much detail as your conscience, emotions, and intellect provide.

Begin now, either on the next few pages of this book, in a journal of your own, or in the *Extraordinary Why Companion Workbook.*

"MERLIN" **YOUR LEGACY**

Write in present tense – you are already there in your future. You have fulfilled your purpose and have achieved your desired legacy! Breathe deeply as you write.

"MERLIN" YOUR LEGACY (CONTINUED)

"MERLIN" **YOUR LEGACY** *(CONTINUED)*

*Now, remain in the future and look backwards toward today. Keep journaling but this time, write in the past tense as you describe **who you were being**, and a few of **the things you did** to break through any obstacles you encountered on your journey to achieve your desired legacy. Keep writing:*

"MERLIN" **YOUR LEGACY** *(CONTINUED)*

If you participated seriously and deeply in that *whole being* exercise, you're off to a great start. Continue this practice in the days ahead. As you do, the picture of the world after you're gone and have fulfilled your purpose will become more real to you.

> *Ongoing backwards glances towards today*
> *from your achieved desired legacy*
> *will help you identify the most useful ABCDs*
> *you need today to move powerfully forward*
> *into your desired future.*

What you've just written flows from your identity – who you see yourself to be at the very core of your being. You tapped into all four dimensions of your being:

- You enlisted your *conscience* as your guide.
- You gave yourself permission to get *emotional* as you worked.
- You got fired up / choked up about those people, projects, and relationships that mean the most to you.
- You put your *intellect* to work in forming the words, sentences, and paragraphs to make coherent sense of all you were experiencing.
- Last, your *physical body* got into action and wrote all that down.

Congratulations!

With that powerful, fulfilling *Legacy* in mind, you're now better prepared than ever before to live into your desired future.

Because of your hard work of introspection and reflection as you've worked your way through this book, you can now *live into your Desired Legacy, from your Desired Legacy.*

We'll end this chapter with two quotes from a couple movie characters who exemplified living from *Extraordinary Why.*

The opening quote of this chapter is from one of my favorite movies: <u>Braveheart.</u> William Wallace, an actual historical figure, truly lived an extraordinary life by anyone's standard. Facing an imminent public death by torture, Wallace unforgettably states:

> *"Every man dies. Not every man really lives!*[viii]*"*

This is just one of the many inspirational lines from that epic film about Wallace, the Scottish Rebel who led an uprising against a tyrannical English King. Wallace was a man who knew his purpose and was willing to die in pursuit of fulfilling it. In so doing, he freed himself to fully live while helping his fellow Scots earn their freedom from tyranny!

This final quote comes from another of my favorite movies: a romantic 'dram-com' called <u>About Time.</u>[ix] Our fictional 'hero' in this film is an ordinary, young British man named Tim Lake who discovered the secret to living life to its fullest. At age 21, he learns from his father that the men in their family have the power to travel back in time. Tim receives this gift as part of his *heritage* and ultimately discovers how to steward his gift very well. It's a delightful film that ends by revealing how ordinary people, like you and me, can live *extraordinary* lives that truly matter to those around us.

Here's Tim's secret:

> *"I just try to live everyday*
> *as if I've deliberately come back to this one,*
> *to enjoy it, as if it was the final full day*
> *of my extraordinary, ordinary life."*
> *– Tim Lake in* <u>About Time</u>

NOTES

i. *A Beautiful Day in the Neighborhood,* directed by Marielle Heller. Written by Noah Harpster & Micah Fitzerman-Blue. Inspired by the article *Can You Say ... Hero* by Tom Junod. Produced by Big Beach Films, Tencent Pictures and TriStar Pictures, Los Angeles, 2019.

ii. *Collateral Beauty,* directed by David Frankel (2016; Los Angeles, CA: New Line Cinema, Village Roadshow Pictures 2017), DVD.

iii. *Hamilton,* Oskar Eustis, Jill Furman, Sander Jacobs, Lin-Manuel Miranda, Jeffrey Seller, Patrick Willingham, Broadway, New York 2015.

iv. Lin-Manuel Miranda/Leslie Odom Jr., "My Shot," Lin-Manuel Miranda, 2015.

v. Lin-Manuel Miranda/Christopher Jackson, "History Has Its Eyes On You," Lin-Manuel Miranda, 2015.

vi. R.M. Fulmer and S. Perret, "The Merlin Exercise: Future by Forecast or Future by Invention." Journal of Management Development 12, no. 6 (1993): 44-52.

vii. TH White, *The Once and Future King* (United Kingdom: Collins, 1958).

viii. William Wallace quote as depicted by Mel Gibson in *Braveheart.* The movie. Directed by Mel Gibson. Written by Randall Wallace. (Icon Entertainment International & The Ladd Company, 1995), DVD.

ix. *About Time,* directed by Richard Curtis (2013; Los Angeles, CA: Translux, Working Title Films 2014), DVD.

Chapter 10

Transformation

"Inner transformation
is God's work – not ours."
– Richard J. Foster

Two worldviews – Two cycles of life

Throughout life, we change.

We change rapidly from the instant we're conceived until the day we're born. Then, from the moment we take our first breath until the day we breathe our last, we continue to change.

Most change in our lives is incidental <u>to</u> *who we are* – change that is additive, or subtractive, to who we already are as a person.

We learn a new skill, a new way of thinking, or behaving that adds something to us. Or, we can lose a skill or capacity we once had.

In either case, we're still the same person. We've just gained something new or lost something once familiar. Nonetheless, there are seasons in our lives when we experience profound change <u>in</u> *who we are*.

Our identity shifts. We just don't grow incrementally – we *transform*.

trans · form

[tran(t)s'fôrm]

VERB

1. make a thorough or dramatic change in the form, appearance, or structure; metamorphose
2. to alter in condition, nature, or character; convert.

Transformational change results in a fundamental shift in our identity – who we are at our core. It affects how we see ourselves or how others view and regard us as humans. Transformation, therefore, alters us in one or more of the four components of our whole being: *physical, intellectual, emotional,* or *spiritual.*

Conception, birth, puberty, maturation, aging, and death are all natural, physical transformations. Elite athletes commit to diet and exercise regimens that also result in dramatic positive *physical* transformation.

Alternatively, make the habitual choice to over-eat and under-exercise and you'll experience a negative physical transformation.

Intellectually, we grow by studying, reading, and gaining new knowledge. Continue on this journey and you'll become a life-long learner – one who is transformed by the ongoing renewal of your mind.

Over-watch mindless TV or spend hours in front of senseless video games and your *intellectual* transformation won't be as positive.

Emotional transformations occur when we fall in love or become a parent, for example. We also develop in *emotionally* positive ways when we embrace forgiveness, make peace with our past, and choose to overlook offenses committed against us.

Hold onto every offense perpetrated against you, and you'll soon transform into an angry, bitter person.

Awakenings, conversions, rebirths, and enlightenments are all words people use to describe various *spiritual* transformations they experience. We can make a habit of regularly dwelling in the presence of our Creator.

We can cultivate a deep, intimate relationship with God – get to know 'him' personally as he is, not how we want him to be. These choices invariably lead to a *spiritual* rebirth.

On the other hand, continually ignore the promptings of your conscience.

Remain consumed by life's urgencies, never set apart time to commune with your Creator, and the *spiritual* transformation you'll experience will inevitably prove highly dissatisfying.

The sum of our attitudes, behaviors, choices, and decisions *(ABCDs)* transform us. For better or worse, we are not the same being at the end of our journey that we were when we began.

It is not nature or nurture that determines your destiny. As you go through the cycle of life, you are assuredly the product of your *ABCDs*.

There are, at least, two different worldviews regarding the transformative cycle of life. One is a *secular* worldview – temporal in nature and, by definition, non-spiritual. The other is overtly *spiritual*.

Here's how the cycle of life looks from a purely *secular* worldview as we go through life's predicable transformations:

The Secular Cycle of Life

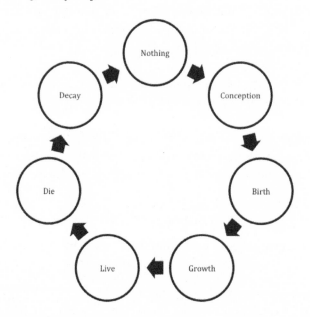

You begin as *nothing* with no identity. Then, you experience formative transformation: *conception*. You develop in your mother's womb until you're again transformed at *birth*. Once becoming an 'air-breather,' you again transform through puberty and *grow* to maturity. Hopefully, you'll embrace your *intellectual* being as you grow. You'll develop mental capacities. You'll also develop *physical* abilities, skills and talents – some of which might make you successful in life. You'll discover what makes you *emotional*, and you'll spend more time doing things that bring positive emotions and fewer negative ones. In maturity, your transformation is largely driven by your *ABCDs*.

You are *"the master of your fate, the captain of your soul,"* as the English poet William Ernest Henley famously penned in his poem *Invictus.*[i]

You live. You die. You decay into dust. You become nothing once again.

Did any of it even matter? This cycle of life is hopeless and meaningless.

Consider this alternative worldview: a *spiritual* cycle.

The Spiritual Cycle of Life

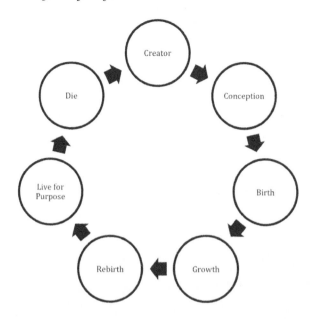

This cycle acknowledges we are inherently *spiritual* beings, in addition to being physical, intellectual, and emotional. Here's how that cycle progresses as we go through life's predictable transformations:

You begin in the heart and mind of your *Creator*. God wills you into existence. He creates you in His own image through *conception* and oversees the transformation in your mother's womb until the moment of your *birth*. As you *physically* grow to maturity, so does your awareness of the other parts of your being: you become aware of your *intellect* and your *emotions*. You also become *spiritually* aware. Your identity as a whole, four-dimensional, being is formed. You sense you were created for a purpose.

Enlisting your *conscience* as your guide, you experience a transformative *rebirth*. You become a new creature, one who *knows* your Creator, personally. You experience and embrace God's Love. This frees you to truly live! You live abundantly, embracing life's delights and joys, and difficulties.

In each circumstance, if you submit your *ABCDs* to your *conscience's* leading, you'll become aware of your Life's Purpose – *Why* you're here.

Then, you're *doing* in the world flows out of your *being* – your *identity*. You fulfill your purpose and your life has mattered.

Your *physical* body will ultimately die. But in this *whole being* cycle of life, your *spiritual* being will not end. You will be reunited with your Creator, for eternity, to fulfill new purposes yet to be revealed!

Two different worldviews: one secular, the other spiritual. Two entirely different ways of viewing this thing called cycle of life. You may subscribe to one of these views or the other. Perhaps neither accurately portrays your worldview. Remember, I said there are *at least* two! The important point to acknowledge is this:

Your worldview will influence your attitudes, behaviors, choices, and decisions throughout your life.
Your legacy is at stake.

Which will you choose?

Will you choose a worldview of life that leads to mere temporal success, or will you choose to live a life that leads to lasting significance?

The choice is entirely yours.

Inspiring others to find their identity

During the fall semester of her sophomore year in college, my daughter, Lauren, came home one weekend very excited.

"Dad," she said animatedly. *"I want to go on another relief trip!"*

"Great! Where are we going this time?" I replied.

"Oh! Sorry. You're not coming on this one." Lauren broke the news to me as gently as she could.

"Oh. That's okay," I said, trying to remain equally as enthusiastic for her as I was before discovering I was to be excluded from this adventure.

"Where are you going this time?" I quickly added.

"There's this group going to Kenya over the winter break," Lauren began. *"Two weeks of serving in a variety of roles: Medical relief work, educational programs, some light construction projects, mission work. For some reason, I just can't get Africa off my heart. I can't fully explain it, but I think I'm supposed to go with them. I'll raise all the funds. Will you take me to the airport the day after Christmas so I can go?"*

"Of course!" I replied, overcome with pride in my rapidly maturing daughter.

Just three months later, our family arrived together at the Charlotte airport to see Lauren off to Africa. This 'kid' who usually didn't come home from college for a weekend without suitcases full of laundry, was standing at the airport with a tiny daypack filled with all her personal needs for the next two weeks. We all stood there in shock!

"Are you sure you're taking enough clothes?" her mother asked.

"Do you have all the necessities?" I added. Both of us obviously worried for her well-being on such a long trip.

"I'm fine Mom and Dad. I promise. Besides, the more we take personally, the less we can carry for the kids we'll be working with."

Lauren received no audible response from either of us. Speech was not an option for me in that moment! A few brief moments, and many hugs later, she was off on her adventure. An adventure with people we knew little about to a faraway continent about which we knew even less.

Faith! Time stood still.

When Lauren returned from that journey, she blogged about her experiences in Africa – the things she saw and did, and the profound impact those experiences had on her. As I read Lauren's words on my screen, I choked up. I never even knew such beautiful, descriptive, compelling words were in her! I let them pour over me as I read them again and again.

Soon, the all-too-familiar pressure built in the sinuses behind my nose and eyes. Tears streamed down my cheeks, and I made no effort to wipe them away. I was in public – on a plane, of course. Yet, I was unashamed. Quite the contrary: I was proud!

My darling firstborn went out into the world – alone. The Third World! Not in ignorance of what loomed ahead for her there, but *despite* the discomfort she knew awaited.

She felt *called,* and she heeded the call. Then, she processed her experiences in a blog for the benefit of others. In that moment, I knew this 'child' of mine was slowly, but surely, finding her own unique *identity* – her voice!

Who will you inspire?

If we achieve *success* in this life but don't invest ourselves in others along the way, our life will not have mattered. We will have wasted this gift called life. If you want your life to matter, if you want to live a life of *significance*, you must invest yourself in *others*. It's that simple.

Ask your conscience this question:

> *Who will I inspire before I die?*

Now, keep just one of those specific people in your mind as you read through the next several pages and learn a process for inspiring others to transform.

We're going to return to our friends at the Welton Academy in the film _Dead Poets Society_,[ii] for one final lesson. Let's 'watch' as Robin Williams shows us _how_ to inspire another to _'find their voice.'_

As the scene opens, it's now Monday morning – time for the boys to read their poems, aloud, in front of the class. One after another, the boys stand and deliver their poems.

Expressing his desire to put an end to young Mr. Anderson's misery and dread, Keating calls on the young man. Sheepishly, the boy looks up. He swallows hard and hesitantly looks up to his teacher. Almost matter-of-factly Anderson declares he didn't do the assignment. He didn't write a poem.

Keating's eyebrows rise on his forehead. Disappointed, but not surprised, by the boy's response, he walks towards him.

When he arrives in front of the lad, he resumes teaching his lesson to the whole class by using poor Mr. Anderson as his example. In a loud voice Keating declares that young Mr. Anderson doesn't think he has anything to contribute to the world. After speaking the boy's worst fear aloud, he then disagrees, saying he believes there's something of great value in him!

With that verbal acknowledgment of faith and belief, Keating continues the process of drawing Anderson's voice out of him. He physically ushers the boy to the front of the class and encourages him to begin by uttering a single word: a loud cry or yell that the class' sage muse, Walt Whitman, calls a 'Barbarian YAWP!'

After several anemic efforts on Anderson's part, Keating finally manages to coax a loud angry 'YAWP' from the boy. Anderson immediately attempts to return to the safety of his seat – but he doesn't get away!

Keating grabs the boy by his shoulders and spins him around, turning his back to the class. He directs his attention to the portraits above the blackboard, telling him he's not done yet and is not going to escape his assignment so easily.

Keating then points directly to the portrait of Walt Whitman and asks the boy what the picture looks like to him. Snapping his fingers to distract him, Keating tells him not to think about it, just answer.

"A ma-ma madman," Anderson stammers.

At this point, Keating steps up his energy even more. He starts walking around the boy in counter-clockwise circles. This movement seems to further disorient Anderson – getting him even more out of his head. Keating presses the boy to describe the madman.

"A crazy madman," Anderson blurts out.

Keating challenges the boy's rather generic response telling him he can do better. He presses him harder until Anderson does, eventually, come up with a truly original description:

"A sweaty-toothed madman!" Anderson finally delivers.

Keating praises him and continues to offer encouragement.

Not wanting to lose the momentum they've built, the teacher tells him to close his eyes. A confused and hesitant Anderson doesn't quite get the idea, so Keating moves in. He places his left hand sideways on the back of the boy's neck, and he covers Anderson's eyes himself using his own right hand. Keating begins to spin the two of them around in a circle as he continues his coaching. He asks the boy to describe what he sees in the darkness now before him.

Tentatively, Anderson completes his first sentence describing the *'sweaty-toothed madman.'* Keating again praises the boy's start and continues to offer coaching suggestions.

After more encouraging words, Keating releases his grip on the boy.

Anderson now faces the classroom directly, but he's oblivious to his positioning as his eyes are firmly shut. Keating backs away giving Anderson space to stand there on his own. The boy continues speaking, gaining confidence as he goes. Keating moves further and further away and crouches down before him as the boy performs.

Ultimately, Anderson produces a powerful poem, filled with emotion that comes from deep within his soul!

Panting and out of breath, Anderson opens his eyes to discover Mr. Keating crouched down before him, hands folded in solemn fashion across his chest. There's a look of deep satisfaction and pride on Keating's face. A long, silent pause hangs in the air as Anderson slowly realizes what he has just done. The teacher and student exchange a meaningful glance at each other as the silence persists. It's palpable.

The camera pans around the classroom. We see similar looks of awe and admiration on the other students' faces as they break into spontaneous, affirming applause – acknowledging Anderson's accomplishment.

Slowly, Keating rises from his squat. He walks up to Anderson, the man. He grabs the back of his head once again with his right hand and pulls him close. Leaning into him with his head practically in contact with Anderson's forehead, Keating gives the final instruction of the lesson:

"Don't you forget this!"

A broad smile emerges across Anderson's face, assuring us that he most certainly will not! Neither, of course, will we.

Immediately, we cut to a scene with Anderson and the whole class out on the soccer field with Keating, their coach. There are no words in the scene, just the visual. Beethoven's *Ode to Joy* choral masterpiece plays on dramatically as the audio background.

How very appropriate!

Now that you've read the description of this powerful scene, you may want to watch if for yourself. Let me encourage you to do just that. In this book, we've 'watched' four different scenes from _Dead Poets Society._ Again, I encourage you to watch the whole film – it's superbly done and is packed with challenging life lessons for us all.

Step-By-Step Guide to Inspiring Those You Lead

Let's 'unpack' the important life lesson from the scene just described. Here's a step-by-step guide for how you can inspire those you lead:

Step 1 – Challenge

The first step did not appear in the movie scene just described. It was actually depicted in the prior clip from the movie. Remember the scene in which Professor Keating gave the boys the assignment?

He instructed them to compose a poem of their own and announced they must speak it – _"Aloud. In front of the class, on Monday."_

Keating knew that assignment terrified shy Mr. Anderson!

That's our first job as a leader: **Challenge your people with big goals** – goals that make them uncomfortable.

We transform outside of our comfort zone – not inside our comfort zone. If we're trying to _transform_ our people – help them become all that they were created to be _(the very definition of transformation)_, then we must make them uncomfortable.

That's Step 1 to inspire someone to transform:

Challenge **them with a goal that's bigger than they think they can achieve.**

Step 2 – Expect & Believe

The second step is depicted right at the beginning of the scene. Keating issued the assignment on Friday. Now, it's Monday. It's time to deliver. Keating walks over to Mr. Anderson, acknowledges he knows the boy is in misery, and offers him the chance to be done with it.

I LOVE that Keating didn't ask *'Why?'* when Anderson replied that he didn't do the assignment. That would have been the worst possible question he could ask! Because then, the student would simply give an excuse, take his zero on the assignment, and he'd be 'off the hook.'

But Keating doesn't ask *'why?'* and that makes everything else that happens in that scene possible.

No, Keating doesn't ask Anderson *'Why?'* he didn't write his poem. It's clear that Keating doesn't much care *'Why?'* What he cares about is *performance* and *transformation*.

Keating is essentially saying to the boy:

'This relationship we have is far too important for us to let <u>unaccountability</u> creep in and spoil it. The assignment was a poem today. I expect you to do it! Get on up here; you are going to perform.'

But Keating also gave the boy the gift of his *belief.* He told the whole class that he *believed* there was something of great value inside Anderson. That's the second half of this very important step:

You need to <u>believe</u> in your people.

Believe in them, even when they let you down. Believe in them, even when they are *unaccountable*. Your people *need* your belief. They will *know* if it's missing. They'll feel it!

So that's Step 2:

<u>*Expect*</u> **them to perform,** <u>*don't accept excuses*</u>**, and** <u>*believe*</u> **in them.**

Step 3 – Create Safety

After Keating finally gets a passionate, truly *'barbaric YAWP'* out of the boy, he blindfolds him and spins him around. This is a delightfully dramatic action (great for a movie!), but what purpose did it serve?

If you've properly set up the challenge in Step 1, then your people are going to feel uncomfortable. Good! That's what you want. However, sometimes if we're too uncomfortable, we become petrified. We're too afraid even to begin.

Young Mr. Anderson was uncomfortable ever since the assignment was issued on Friday afternoon. By the time he got to Monday morning and it was time to deliver in front of the class, he was terrified … too afraid even to speak.

This is not uncommon. It's often been noted that fear of public speaking is one of the greatest human fears, often ranked higher than fear of death. So much so, that at funerals many people would rather be 'in the box' than delivering the eulogy!

All kidding aside, speaking in public does create a great deal of anxiety in people, especially in those who are shy or painfully self-conscious. This is true because when we speak up and use our 'voice' in a public setting, we are standing out. Our ego is at risk, and our ego is incredibly self-protective.

Keating knew was the case for Mr. Anderson. No shy, self-conscious student wants to stand out in front of the class. They want to be anonymous, to fade into the background. By being up in front of the class, Anderson was the sole center of attention in front of all his peers, and it frightened him.

It was the perfect storm for the boy. He was face-to-face with his worst fear. He couldn't even start. So Keating created *safety* for him. By blindfolding Anderson and spinning him around, Keating distracted him from those things in his reality that caused him so much anxiety. He essentially took his peers out of the picture for Mr. Anderson.

They're not even here! It's just you and me. You're safe.

Safe for what? Why did it need to be safe?

What did Anderson believe would happen if he began speaking publicly? Keating gave us that answer right up front – *that there was nothing of value inside of him.* That he was a failure. So, Keating created *safety for failure.*

Do you have any failures in your past?

- Something you did or said, that you wish you hadn't?
- Some lapse of integrity, perhaps?
- Some risk you could have taken, but you were too afraid, so you played it safe and missed out on a big opportunity?

If you're human, and at all self-aware, now would be the time to say:

'Yes! Of course!'

Did that failure end you? Of course not! If it did, you wouldn't be reading this right now. On the contrary, that failure, all your failures, helped make you into the person you are today! You needed those failures to become who you are.

Your failures don't define who you are, but they certainly helped shape you *into* who you are. Whether your failures made you 'bitter' or better' was, and is, a choice. Either way, your failures, and what you chose to do with them, were instrumental in your development as a human being.

Here's a powerful thought:

> *We don't make mistakes. Our mistakes make us!*

In our *hearts*, we sense this to be true. But, while it makes sense *intellectually*, our ego doesn't want us to admit when we fail. It encourages us to hide our mistakes, cover them up, rather than own them and acknowledge that we're not perfect.

Perhaps, you may be like me: a *recovering perfectionist*. If so, you might operate as if it's your job as a leader to create an environment in which your people *won't* fail. That it's your job as a parent to ensure that your children *don't* fail.

No! Our people *need* their failures. Our children need *their* failures.

Our job, as leaders who love them, who want what's best for them, is *to create a safe environment in which they can fail* without it being catastrophic, without that failure being fatal ... ending them.

So, this is the third step to inspire someone to find their identity and fulfill their potential in the world:

Create a *safe environment* in which they can *fail*.

Step 4 – Educate & Coach

Professor Keating is a teacher, a trainer of sorts. Teaching and training are forms of putting *your* voice into someone else:

Let me teach you how to do it. Do it like this. Not like that.

That's *me*, putting *my* voice into *my* student. Teaching/training is a matter of showing a particular way to do things and a way not to do things. It's more about eliminating options than it is about opening up possibilities.

There is a way, and I will show you the way.

Let me be clear: I'm not saying there's anything wrong with teaching and training. As we learn and grow as humans, it's necessary for us to be taught and trained in many things.

There are many skills and tasks that leaders must teach their employees to do. Parents must teach their children how to behave and how not to behave. Even so, when it comes to helping, encouraging, and inspiring others to *find their voice* and become all they were meant to be, a different skill set is required. Keating knew this!

As he was working with his student in this scene, at one point, he turns the boy's back to the classroom. He keeps it safe for him by taking his peers/fears out of the picture. Then he points up at the portrait of Walt Whitman and prompts him to speak: *'you describe him,'* and *'give him action.'* He guides him by asking a question: *"What kind of madman?"*

In that moment, Keating shifted out of the role of Teacher/Trainer – he became an Educator/Coach.

Education is about encouraging others to think for themselves. It's not about shutting down options. *Education* is about opening up possibilities. *Coaching* is not about rigorous training in the way things *should* be done.

> *Coaching is helping an individual*
> *find their own unique way of doing –*
> *a way of doing that flows from their unique being.*

Education and Coaching are not about shoving your voice into someone else. Education and Coaching are about *pulling someone else's unique voice out of them!*

You ask questions, you offer promptings and suggestions, but the end product (the poem … the performance) is theirs and theirs alone.

That's Step 4 in our process:

Educate & Coach them to draw *their* voice out of them.

Step 5 – Encourage & Give Space

When the coaching began, Keating was in close proximity to Mr. Anderson. On several occasions, he was physically touching him – lifting him up by his shoulders, hands over his eyes and on the back of his head, spinning him around.

Then, at one point in the scene, Keating backed away from the boy. When? Right after Anderson had started to speak. He started to use his voice. Not until then did Keating back away. Once he started to perform, Keating praised him and *encouraged* him verbally.

Your people need your encouragement as much as they need your belief. *Encouragement* is just the 'business-appropriate' word for *love*. Love your people! They will respond accordingly. Remember, Love is the greatest *why* of all!

After he *encouraged* the boy, he gave him space. *He backed away.* It was a genius move. It returned the boy to a place where he could keep going. It was exactly the *encouragement* he needed at the time he needed it. The rest of the lines came out of the boy while he was standing all on his own. His eyes remained shut – he stood alone in front of the class. He delivered his own original poem! No additional coaching was required. Keating moved further and further away. He even crouched down – he got physically small.

That's the final part of Step 5:

Once your people start performing, get out of the way!

You don't have to do this. You can micromanage the process if you'd like, to 'ensure' they don't fail. You can critique them to death, which will rob them of the experience of finding their own voice. OR, like a jockey 'gives a horse its head' in a race to just let it run, you too can allow your people to step out and run. They'll either succeed wonderfully or fail fabulously! Either way, it won't matter; they'll be finding their own identity in the process!

So that's the fifth, and final, obligatory step in the process:

Encourage **them along the way and** *get out of the way***.**

Step 6 – Enjoy Significance *(Optional)*

There is one more step in this process, but it's optional.

Did you notice the description of the 'deep look of satisfaction' on Keating's face at the end of the scene? Did you notice how Mr. Anderson and some of the other students in the class shared a similar kind of look? It's 'OK' to enjoy the moment! You will have been *significant* in the life of another person. You will have inspired them to find their voice, their identity, and become who they were created to be.

Frankly, not only is it 'OK' to enjoy the moment, hunger for more! Desire "20% more" of that *significance* in the time you have remaining!

Here's a recap of the process:

Six Steps to Inspiring Others

1 – Challenge them with a goal bigger than they think achievable.

2 – Expect them to perform, don't accept excuses, believe in them.

3 – Create a safe environment in which they can fail.

4 – Educate and Coach them to draw their voice out of them.

5 – Encourage them along the way and get out of the way.

6 – Enjoy the significance!

"Transformation without work and pain, without suffering, without a sense of loss, is just an illusion of true change."
— *William Paul Young*

True *transformation* is a process – a painful process. The old *self* must die, so the new *self* can emerge. Our ego doesn't like the thought of its death, so we tend to resist the process.

Yet, we cannot truly become all we were meant to be if we don't die to who we were before we found our voice.

Only when we throw off our need for emotional comfort and safety are we positioned to transform anew. Once we experience *transformation* for ourselves, it's only natural to want others to experience it for themselves.

We cannot do it for them. We cannot spare them the pain that accompanies the process. But we can become coaches that assist, inspire, and guide them along the way.

Don't let your discomfort with challenging others and holding them accountable rob others of the joy of transforming into who they were created to be!

We've nearly completed our journey together. The final chapter is one I promise you will never forget. It will serve as a powerful illustration of why the work you've done as we've traveled together through this book is of crucial importance. This work matters. It's significant – to you and to the world around you!

"Transformed people transform people."
– Richard Rohr

NOTES

i. William Ernest Henley, "Invictus," Poetry Foundation, accessed October 30, 2019, https://www.poetryfoundation.org/poems/51642/invictus

ii. *Dead Poet's Society*, directed by Peter Weir (1989; Los Angeles, CA: Touchstone Pictures, 1998), DVD.

Chapter 11

Leading From Your Extraordinary Why

"Those who don't know history are destined to repeat it."
— *Edmund Burke*

As we've seen throughout our journey together, *conscience* plays a crucial role in connecting individual people to purpose.

But, does *conscience* exist only in individuals? Or is there such a thing as a *collective conscience?* Does an organization possess a *conscience* of its own? If so, what practices might a leader employ to help an organization cultivate an intimate relationship with that resource to ensure their culture remains healthy — to guarantee the organization finds its *Extraordinary Why*, shares it with the world, and becomes all it was meant to be?

The *Why* of an organization

As I write this chapter, I'm flying home from Belfast, Northern Ireland. There, I spoke to a large group of CEOs about leadership. Of course, we discussed how to lead organizations to *success*. More memorably, our conversation centered on how to lead organizations to *significance* — about the leader's responsibility to ensure their organization is a force for good and contributes positively to the world.

Ironically, the conference was held at the Titanic Museum in downtown Belfast. I spoke from the steps of the Grand Staircase in the Titanic Suite, an imposing replica of the opulent main lounge of the White Star Line's ill-fated ship.

The significance of the setting was apparent to all as I posed the question:

Does the concept of Legacy apply to organizations?

Many heads nodded affirmatively, and several hands went up at once. Without exception, the leaders all agreed that *legacy* applied to organizations. As we dug into the matter further, an interesting consensus emerged:

> *An organization's 'legacy' is created over time.*
> *It lives in the minds and hearts of those that encounter it.*
> *Not just after it 'dies' –*
> *But <u>after each interaction people have with it</u>*
> *while it 'lives.'*

How do people *feel* after interacting with us as a company? Did we help them feel valued? Respected? Cared for as dignified individuals of inestimable worth as fellow humans? Or, did they feel used? Did they feel as if we viewed and treated them as a means to an end – a resource to be exploited for profit?

That's similar to the legacy of an individual isn't it? In both cases, legacy lives in the minds and hearts of those that encounter us – after we're gone, of course, but also after every experience they have with us. The attitudes, behaviors, choices, and decisions we make while we're operating determine the legacy we leave in our wake – as individuals and as companies.

Clearly, *Legacy* applies to both individuals and organizations.

But, what about this idea that an organization as a whole possesses a *conscience* – a collective conscience – is that possible?

Consider this final story.

Work will set you free[i]

When the time came time for my middle child's one-on-one trip with me, my daughter Kaitlyn chose a different kind of trip. She said:

"Hey Dad! There's this youth camp in the mountains of Slovakia. I want to go to Slovakia and teach my high school peers how to speak English."

Her trip, her agenda, so I wasn't about to argue! The next summer, we got on a plane and flew to Eastern Europe. It was a wonderful experience to watch my daughter teach her peers the lessons she had developed.

In my recollection, it seemed all the lessons somehow involved me being the butt of a joke. The kids had a great time laughing hysterically at my expense, all the while learning English!

The experience proved to be a formative one for my daughter too. It stretched her. Took her out of her comfort zone and helped her to discover her identity. Her proud father's heart melted in the process, of course.

At the end of our time there in Slovakia, Kaitlyn and I had three days remaining before our flight home. I looked at the map and noticed that just to the north of Slovakia was this little country called Poland.

I pointed it out:

"Hey Kaitlyn, your grandmother was from Poland. You want to drive up there and see the land of our heritage?"

"Yeah Dad! Let's go!" Kaitlyn enthusiastically responded.

We drove down out of the mountains of Czech Republic and entered the flat grasslands of southern Poland. There, we came to what proved to be a literal and proverbial fork in the road. Krakow, our intended destination was close. But a short detour would take us to Auschwitz-Birkenau. A brief glance at each other and we immediately knew our travels were about to include an unplanned stop.

Allow me to take you there.

Auschwitz has been preserved largely like it was found when it was liberated on January 27th, 1945 by the Soviets. Curved, concrete posts rise up out of the ground. Barbed wire is strung all along them, surrounding the entire perimeter of the enormous compound.

Railroad tracks run right through the center of the Birkenau complex. Between the tracks and the stark brick administration buildings stands a giant, iron sign under which all who enter must walk.

Upon the sign, those three infamous German words are emblazoned for all eternity: *"Arbeit Macht Frei."* Literally translated, it means: *"Work Will Set You Free."*

During the height of the death camp's operations, trains would regularly arrive on those tracks from throughout Europe. An SS officer positioned at the end of the platform would greet each train. He'd evaluate 'the cargo' as it approached him.

If you were a woman or a child and looked as if they could extract no labor from you, you'd be sent to the left – straight to the gas chambers and on into the crematorium. You'd be dead, processed, and disposed of within hours of your arrival at the camp.

That's how efficient the *machine* was by the end of the war.

If you were able-bodied and looked as if they could extract some labor from you, you'd be sent the other way: to the right – to the labor camps. It didn't necessarily matter if they sent you that way; you'd still be dead within three to four months of your arrival. That was the average life expectancy at Auschwitz.

At one point on the modern-day tour of Auschwitz, you enter the barracks. There, you witness the unbelievably disreputable 'living' conditions one human can subject another human to by failing to make *conscience-based decisions* in life and business.

The most disturbing part of the tour?

You walk down some steps into a large room. Once the last member of your group enters, they slam shut the iron door, through which you entered. As your eyes slowly adjust to the darkness in which you find yourself, you gradually become cognizant that the only openings in this room are two vents on the ceiling – one at either end of the room. These were the very vents through which they'd drop the Zyklon B.

Twenty minutes later, three thousand people at a time would be piled up in two heaps of naked bodies. The last people to perish in the chamber climb atop the bodies of the first victims to expire. They'd try to reach the top to gasp a few lasts breaths of air from the very vents through which the gas that killed them entered.

In a magnificent design of engineering efficiency, over on the sidewall of the room, were large, iron doors. The doors unlatch from the backside enabling them to slide open.

Behind the doors – the ovens.

After the toxic air cleared from the space, workers would enter. They'd pull the twisted bodies from the heaps and toss them into the ovens, two at a time.

Why two at a time?

They burn faster that way. You learn gruesome details like that in a place like Auschwitz.

We exited the crematorium, and I hit my knees in the dirt and wept.

Sobbed.

Overcome with emotion, a flood of memories swept over me – from my own past. I recalled a leadership development exercise I had experienced about a decade before.

I worked for an oil company at the time. The company had outsourced leadership development to places with a world-class reputation for developing leaders – Harvard Business School, Stanford's School of Business, etc. The experience that came flooding back to me was the time I spent at Cambridge University in England.

My work team completed a prescribed business simulation. The instructions were simple:

"You are the leadership team of a manufacturing company. It's your job to run the most successful company you possibly can.

Every hour we'll give you data. Process the data. Run the business. Make decisions. Be successful. That's why we're paying you."

Apparently, we performed well. At the end of the day, the course leaders encouraged us: *"As far as we know, nobody has ever run a more profitable company through this simulation."*

We had nailed it! We gave each other high fives. We celebrated!

The celebration ended abruptly when the instructors opened the doors on the background of the companies they had used to create our simulation. Sadly, it had been based upon actual companies. Dozens of companies that slowly but surely had ultimately become complicit in the Nazi War Machine.

Complicit to the point that one company was manufacturing Zyklon B. Another company was building gas chambers. One company was *running* Auschwitz!

What?

How does this happen? How does a group of business leaders become complicit in *evil* to the point that they're *running a death camp?*

Here's how: one economic decision at a time.

"Where are you going to build the next manufacturing plant?"

"Here are three Profit & Loss statements (P&Ls) each describing a possible location for the new plant. Take your pick. Crunch the numbers and make your decision."

This, of course, we do. In the analysis, we discover that if we build the plant at one particular location, we'd have a really low Cost of Goods Sold.

That's good for business! That one looks like the best location for our new plant.

The 'labor' item on that P&L was zero. That would have been a good time to ask a *conscience-based* question like:

"Hey, shouldn't you have to pay your people something? People don't work for free, do they?"

Apparently, they did at this camp: it was located right next door to a concentration camp. There's an unlimited supply of free labor.

We didn't ask. We didn't care. In our simulation, we built a plant right there at that location. That gave us a low manufacturing cost – now and into the foreseeable future. It was clearly the smartest business decision.

"Why do you have to join 'The Party' in order to get the contract?"

"Oh please … make no mistake. Joining 'The Party' is completely optional. Optional! Look, here are three different contracts – you can acquire this new business with minimal hassle. You can get any one, or all three, without joining 'The Party.'"

Of course, we dug into numbers, the specifics terms and conditions of each contract. We discovered on page sixteen, in the fine print, that if we got those alternative contracts, they would dry up in just two to three months. Further, those other contracts weren't even all that significant at the outset.

"You want the big contract? The government contract? The contract that grows over time? Afraid you're going to have to join 'The Party' to get that contract."

Now, they didn't call it the Nazi Party. That would have been obvious. The Party was called something benign. Neutral. It seemed like The Party would be a perfectly legitimate partner with whom to do business.

Another logical business choice! Yet none of us asked any of these kinds of questions:

"What is 'The Party' doing in the culture?"
"What do they stand for in society?"
"What are their core values?"
"Do they consistently act in accordance with their stated values?"
"What impact are they having on the world around them?"

If we had just asked any single *conscience-based* question, we would have received a sheet of paper describing exactly whom we were joining; who we were *becoming* by aligning the interests of our company with the interests of The Party.

But we didn't ask. We joined.

It was a smart business decision to join. The result? Our top line revenues soared. Our cost of goods sold remained low. Our net income – our profits – were huge!

And we had become Nazis.

At the end of the simulation, there wasn't a dry eye in that room at Cambridge.

We were given a simple, specific goal:

"Run the most <u>successful</u> company you possibly can."

What we heard, to a person, was:

"Run the most <u>profitable</u> company you possibly can."

We had absolutely equated high *profits* with high *success* on an unqualified basis. The only way you can do that is by leaving your *conscience* at the door.

Does an organization possess a *collective conscience?*

It may not be identical to the *conscience* of an individual, but that day we all agreed that our *corporate culture* as a whole was lacking. It was woefully inadequate to address the challenges we faced. In our culture, we valued profits and performance over human life and dignity.

None of us, as individuals, was satisfied with our *collective* choice.

All that experience came flooding back to me on the hallowed ground of Auschwitz that day. I was overcome with emotion. I got up from the dirt, walked straight to the bookstore at Auschwitz, and asked:

"Do you have Man's Search for Meaning by Viktor Frankl? His book has been on my reading list for nearly thirty years. I think it's time it came off my list and got into my head … maybe my heart … changed me a little bit?"

"You're in luck! We have one copy left."

Forty Polish Zloty later, that copy became mine.

The quotes and concepts already delineated in this book are contained in Frankl's landmark masterpiece – that triumph of the human spirit!

It's a *must-read* for every human.

The meaning of life

Someone once inquired what question Albert Einstein would ask God if he had the opportunity to do so. His initial reply was, *"How did the universe start? Because everything after that is just math."*

After some additional consideration, he revised his answer. *"Instead,"* he continued on, *"I would ask 'Why was the universe created?' Because then I would know the meaning of my own life."*

The highlight of Frankl's incredibly inspirational book, from that unbelievably dark place, is his legacy to the world.

In essence, Frankl says:

'So many people go around asking: What's the meaning of life? Tell me what this is supposed to be all about, and I will gladly organize my life, my company, my family in such a way that I'm sure to give life meaning. Tell me, and I will do it!'

Frankl's legacy to the world is this:

> *"What's the meaning of life?*
>
> *No! You do NOT get to ask this question.*
>
> *This is the question life asks you.*
> *Life demands an answer.*
> *Each day, you answer that question."*

Personal, *conscience-based leadership* of ourselves is essential if we are to live individual lives of meaning and purpose. We must occasionally step back from the activity of life and reflect upon the big questions:

- Why am I here on Earth?
- What must I achieve while I'm here?
- Where am I currently off-track?
- What corrections do I need to make today?
- Why do any of these things truly matter in the first place?

The answers we receive from our conscience give us the opportunity to adjust course. According to what we hear back from our guidance system, we can alter our *ABCDs*. This is the process you've worked your way through in this book. It's the secret to living a life of meaning and contribution that will prove deeply satisfying to you in your final hours.

Ultimately, we're ALL responsible for answering that question for ourselves. Personally.

What will the meaning of my life be? Through our *ABCDs* we all answer that question. Through *your* *ABCDs* YOU are currently answering that very question ... today!

Here, I assert that not just individuals, but organizations, bear that same responsibility. Companies, not-for-profits, governments, religious, and educational institutions – all ultimately come face-to-face with the consequences of their decisions.

So, they too have a moral responsibility to regularly ask themselves these same kinds of questions:

- *Why* do *we* exist as an organization?
- What do *we* stand for?
- What do *we* refuse to compromise along the way?
- Where are *we* currently off-track?
- How must we correct course?

We live in precarious times. Now, more than ever before, we're aware of this. We live in times that require *leaders of significance* to stand up and engage their organizations in deep conversations to clarify and live out their humanity as a collective. Of course, as the leader of an organization, you don't have to do so. It's a choice. You can choose to lead your organization doing business as usual, ignoring these deeper questions.

Beware! If you make *that* choice, just as Thaddeus Stevens famously said in the movie *Lincoln:*

"That internal compass that should direct your corporate soul toward justice might just ossify in your heart."

Then, you too can become complicit in evil, *even* without intending to do so.

How do you live with that?

How do you die with that on your conscience?

There's only one way to avoid that pitfall.

Aleksandr Solzhenitsyn, the Soviet dissident and survivor of the Gulags once said:

"It would be so easy if the problem of good and evil could be resolved simply by finding this group of evildoers ... rounding them up and doing away with them once and for all. But the problem of good and evil is that the line that divides the two runs right through the center of each human heart."

Dare I add:

"... through every organizational soul."

How do you navigate waters that treacherous?

Cultivate an intimate, honest, authentic relationship with your conscience. Individually, and collectively, within your culture as an organization. Consult with your conscience regularly. Ensure it's well-calibrated and steering you, and the organization you lead, rightly.

Don't forget the good news that Frankl teaches us:

You are not Pavlov's Dog!

You get to *choose* the meaning of your life. *You* get to *choose* the *legacy* you will leave behind. *You* get to *choose* the *purpose* your family, your organization will fulfill in the world.

Choose wisely!

Your final hours

There's a delightful film, a documentary, produced by Viktor Frankl's grandson, Alexander Vesely. It's called *Viktor & I.*" You can find it online at this link: http://www.viktorandimovie.com. As we conclude our epic journey, I leave you with this final cinematic gift:

In the film, Vesely documents some of the final moments of Viktor's life. Frankl was 92 years old.

Given his advanced age and deteriorating health, it was apparent that his passing was near. His family had travelled from far and wide to be with him. As he was being rushed into the operating room for a coronary bypass operation to restore blood flow to his heart, Frankl was lucid and alert. In a loud, clear, cheerful voice he suddenly exclaimed to the family, doctors, and specialists gathered 'round:

"The situation lacks tragedy!"

There was nothing sad or tragic for Frankl in that moment. He had seen 'sad.' Frankl had lived in tragedy and sadness for years. In this, his final moment, however, there was nothing sad or tragic at all.

It was as if to say:

I've lived the life of meaning and purpose
I've chosen for myself.
I'm ready to go home to meet my Creator.

That's a pretty good way to live. It's not a bad way to die.

May it be so for us all!

Closing thoughts

If you think of yourself as a mere island, living by yourself, <u>for</u> yourself, you will be here today, gone tomorrow and no one will notice, or even care, that you're gone. You will have lived, you will have died, and, at best, you will have simply *not mattered.*

At worst, not only will you have failed to contribute to society in any meaningful way, you quite possibly may have been complicit in evil, either with or without intent. Either way, your motives will not matter; your resulting legacy will remain intact, in spite of them.

But if choose to live apart from self, and connected to others, connected to the *heritage* that spawned you, to the community that surrounds you, to your *circumstances,* to the *needs of others* around you, to *the Source* that imagined, formed and breathed life into your very being, for *purposes* far greater than anything you could ever ask or imagine on your own, THEN you will have truly lived a life worth living.

A *significant* life. A truly *extraordinary* life.

You will have offered back to the world the gift that *only you* could have given. You will have left a legacy that will matter ... for eternity.

The choice is yours and yours alone:

What meaning will <u>you</u> give to this life?

What purpose will you fulfill in the world in exchange for this Gift of Life that's been entrusted to you?

What will your verse be?

"We have come to know man as he really is.
After all, man is that being who invented
the gas chambers of Auschwitz;
however, he is also that being,
who entered those gas chambers upright,
with the Lord's prayer or the Shema Yisrael on his lips."
— Viktor Frankl[iii]

NOTES

i. Much of this story is captured in the TEDx Talk I gave at Grand Canyon University on Feb 23rd, 2018 called *Conscience – Connecting to Purpose and Avoiding Evil.* You can watch it at this link:

https://www.youtube.com/watch?v=2x0S0eIb8GA

ii. *Viktor & I*, directed by Alexander Vesely (2011; West Hollywood, CA: Noetic Films, 2011), DVD.

iii. Viktor Frankl, *Man's Search for Meaning* (Boston, MA: 2006). First published in German in 1946 under the title *Ein Psycholog erlebt das Konzentrationslager.* Original English edition published by Beacon Press. 2008 UK Edition published by Rider, an imprint of Ebury Publishing, a Random House Group company. Copyright © 1959, 1962, 1984, 1992, 2004 by Viktor E. Frankl. Use by permission of the Estate of Viktor Frankl.

Personal Note

It is my personal belief that we are each uniquely designed and created in the image of God — first in His heart and mind, and then physically here on Earth into this temporal construct of *Time;* for the brief period we call *Life;* for *Purposes* known only to Him.

The *extraordinary* thing is this: God the Father, Creator of all things, desires personal relationship with us and wants to reveal His purposes for us, directly to us! He loves us immensely, *craves* intimacy with us, and is willing to share all of who He is with us, His creatures!

But, to discern God's ways and purposes, we must be willing to regularly spend time with Him. Unhurried time to pursue Him, listen to His voice, learn from Him, and accept the gift of meaning He freely gives.

It is my earnest hope and prayer that as you actively engage with that spiritual part of your being, your *conscience,* that your relationship with God will grow ever more intimate, real, and authentic. In so doing, that you will discover and fulfill your purpose and live an *extraordinary life of significance,* exceedingly beyond all you could ever ask or imagine!

About The Author

Brett Pyle is a transformational speaker whose programs have inspired tens of thousands of people around the world. An expert at working with organizations to unleash the full potential of their people, Brett helps them connect to their purpose and lead from their *Extraordinary Why*.

After graduating from Engineering School at the University of Virginia, Brett launched into his thirty-year global career in business. He began with Andersen Consulting before serving in numerous senior executive roles for oil giants Amoco and BP. In those roles, he attended Executive Education Programs at Harvard Business School, Stanford's Graduate School of Business, and Cambridge University in the U.K.

Following a brief stint as a technology startup partner, Brett spent the next decade leading CEO Peer Advisory Boards for Vistage Worldwide. While serving as a Vistage Chair, Brett developed his own proprietary model of *Conscience-Centered Coaching™*. Now, he trains professional executive coaches worldwide with Blackaby Ministries International and selects just a few CEOs and senior leaders to personally coach.

Along the journey that's taken him to over 70 countries on six continents, Brett's discovered *we're all created for a purpose and gifted with unique skills, ideas and passions that the world desperately needs!*

Today, Brett speaks and inspires over 100 times each year — delivering keynotes and conducting workshops and retreats around the globe — building bridges that connect people to their purpose to deliver breakthrough results that truly matter to the world.

When he's not on the road, Brett lives in Greenville, South Carolina with Jeanne, his wife of 30 years. They have three adult children: Lauren (married to Stephen), Kaitlyn, and Jonathan. They all share a passion for playing games, hiking, and traveling to new and exciting places!

How to Book Brett to Speak

Want to help others find, live, & lead from their *Extraordinary Why*? Brett would love to help you! Connect with him personally to explore how a workshop, keynote, or retreat might serve you, your organization, or your association:

Speaking website: www.brettpyle.com

Author website: www.extraordinarywhy.com

Brett's blog: www.extraordinarywhy.com/blog

LinkedIn: linkedin.com/in/brettpyle

Twitter: twitter.com/btpyle

Email: bp@extraordinarywhy.com

Phone: 864-421-4934